First published in Great Britain by
Ward Lock Limited, 8 Clifford Street,
London W1X 1RB. 1986

© Brown Wells and Jacobs Limited, London. 1986

Written by George Hostler
Illustrations by Mike Peterkin
Designed by Graham Brown
Typesetting by Words & Pictures Limited
Colour originated by RCS Graphics Limited
Printed and Bound by Mandarin Offset Marketing (H.K.) Ltd.
Printed in Hong Kong

British Library Cataloguing in Publication Data

Hostler, George
    Knatty Knits.
    1. Knitting 2. Dressmaking—Pattern
design
    I. Title II. Peterkin, Mike
    646.4'070   TT820

    ISBN 0-7063-6441-4

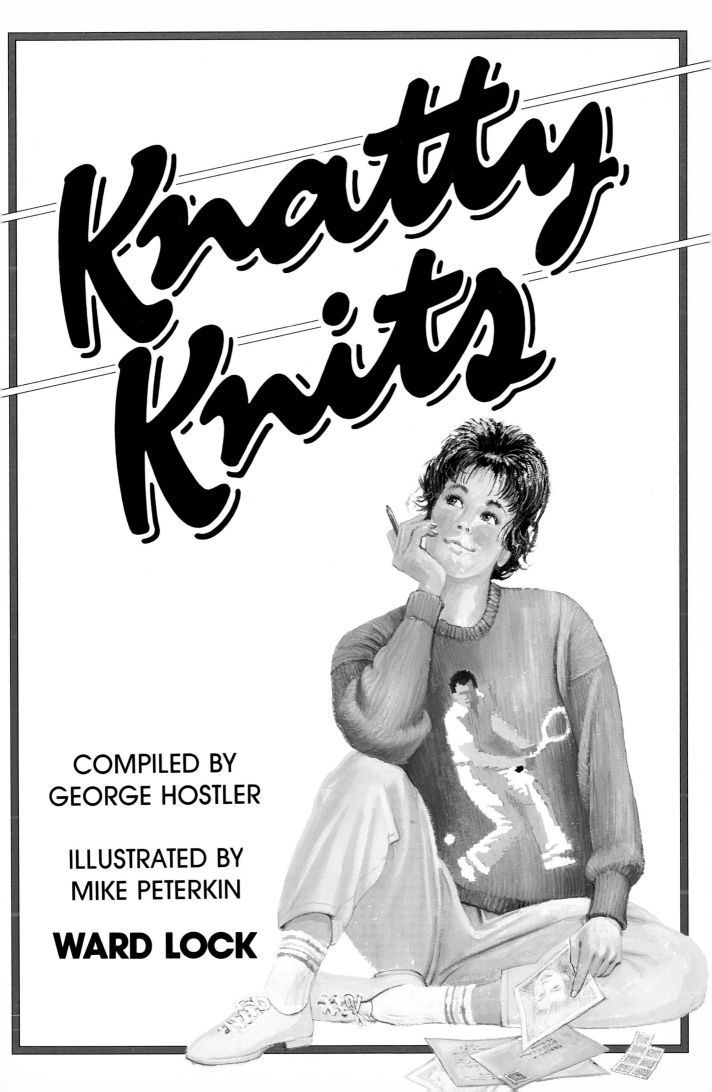

Knatty Knits

COMPILED BY
GEORGE HOSTLER

ILLUSTRATED BY
MIKE PETERKIN

WARD LOCK

Introduction

Knatty Knits is a book for all those knitters, would be knitters or friends of knitters who have always wanted a sweater or item of knitwear which is truly their own. Personalised 'picture knits' can be purchased from specialist knitwear shops – I supply some of them myself – but this can be an unnecessarily expensive business for someone who has the skills and abilities to produce designs for themselves. In Knatty Knits I have set out guidelines which will enable anyone with enthusiasm to work out and draft their own designs and pictures to add to favourite knitting patterns.

I am sure every reader will have, at some time, experienced the exasperation of a fruitless search for that 'special' pattern to suit a tennis playing friend, a football fan, a car fanatic or whatever. Perhaps you have only wanted to add a name or initials to a simple sweater. Well, Knatty Knits is the book for you. In the following pages you will find step by step instructions on how to create your own motif or picture and draw it out as a knitting chart.

Included in the book, as a springboard for your own creative efforts, are detailed patterns for seven classic knitted garments and over 30 picture graphs for use in a variety of yarns. Four alphabets in four different styles, and hints on their layout, round off the knitting graphs.

There is advice for the hand knitter and the machine knitter on how to apply the graphs and handle picture knitting techniques.

Once you have produced that first personalised sweater, don't be surprised if you find yourself inundated with orders and requests from family and friends – so get knitting!

Contents

Creative Hints

The main purpose in putting this book together is to enable any knitter or knitwear enthusiast to adapt, add personal flair and individual character to existing patterns. Creating garments from scratch can be a daunting prospect for even an experienced knitter. Adding your own touches, be it a stripe, a name or a complete design onto an available pattern is well within the scope of anyone with enthusiasm.

The following pages will, hopefully, encourage and explain clearly how to achieve a professional, 'shop bought' look to your endeavours, no matter what the level of your artistic skills.

The ready drawn graphs in the book are there to be used but here is how to go about creating your own designs and pictures.

The designs in the book have been assembled under different headings: Pop, Pets, Events etc. These headings in themselves indicate different areas that you might explore. Create designs for yourself which reflect your interests, hobbies or obsessions.

You don't have to be a talented draughtsman to recreate the images and feel of the subject you wish to depict. If you are interested in something you probably already have magazines, pictures, posters and all manner of source material which can be used.

COLOURS AND STRIPES

Even in terms of stripes and colour changes an amazing amount of inspirational subject matter is easily come by.

For instance, if you want to knit something for a B.M.X. or cycling enthusiast, be it yourself or someone you know, then a quick flick through relevant magazines will show you whole ranges of colour change preferences. Look at the way the cyclists' clothing and protective outfits are coloured and marked. Sleeves are a different colour to the body. Cuffs and welts are contrasting. The body might be divided into three or four bands of clashing colour. Sleeves can be knitted sideways to divide the colour down the arm – the arrangements are limitless. Take tips from the pictures you see and don't be afraid to copy the extravagant colour combinations.

The sporting world is probably the easiest area in which to find source material for colour and pattern arrangements. But just a little more imagination on your part will enable you to adapt the 'feel' for colour and texture which is associated with any subject. Hi fi, cameras, computers and related hi tech images all, for instance, enjoy a common language in black and silver with only touches of primary colour – knit the front of your music centre. Cars and motorcycles use wonderful metallic colours with trim in black and chrome. Explore this with a liberal use of metallic and primary coloured yarns.

The proportions of the stripes and bands you see are just as important as the colour and texture. An elegant example of this can be found looking at a J.P.S. team Formula One racing car. It is an all black car edged round its contours with a double gold line, one a little thicker than the other. You can trim your knitted garment in exactly the same way. An all black sweater with metallic gold (lurex) lines on the edges of welt, cuffs and neck. Use the alphabets in the book to emblazon your own name across your chest.

THE MOTIF OR DESIGN

When you are tackling an actual picture or motif it still isn't necessary to demonstrate great drawing skills. If you can draw or get someone to draw for you then obviously your task will be that much easier, but the instructions, as outlined, can be used to adapt any picture, photograph or drawing you might have. When looking for inspiration, again, as outlined earlier, search through as much pictorial material as you can. Don't hesitate to take your own photographs or delve through your own snap album. Try to find something clear to work from but at the same time look for unusual angles and movement in the pictures. All too often interesting subjects are rendered in a static way. Even if you are just trying to get a picture of the family dog on your sweater try to get something which depicts the way he sits or moves, not just a sideways view or full face. Also try to depict something a bit unusual. 'Picture knits' usually conjure up in one's mind a cuddly animal, rows of sheep or a tree-lined landscape. These are all very well, but it can be very rewarding to succeed with something a little more daring.

STARTING THE DESIGN

You will probably have decided what sort of garment you want before starting on the design or motif you are going to incorporate. Bear in mind that the finer the yarn used the more detail you will be able to show. A chunky knit has huge stitches and you will have to settle for a simple, bold design. On a 4 ply garment the stitches are small and there are lots of them, so you can tackle a very detailed design. A quick check through the graphs already drawn in the book will demonstrate what I mean. For the hand knitter, chunky is of course, the quickest to

knit. The 4 ply garments take longer for the hand knitter but are ideal for the machine knitter. I have included rather more 4 ply graphs in the book than any others simply because they can be used by both types of knitter.

The materials you will require for preparing your own knitting charts are: a 'soft' pencil for drawing; a rubber for endless adjustments; a ruler; a few coloured crayons; tracing paper and graph paper for your finished pattern. The tracing (transparent) paper and graph paper can be obtained from almost any good art materials shop. Graph paper is printed in a variety of measured squares but the easiest to use is marked in inches, subdivided into tenths of an inch and this is the type you should purchase.

SIZING THE DESIGN

Before you can copy your original picture or drawing onto the graph paper you must decide upon its size and how it will fit onto the garment.
The easiest method of sizing a single motif for your garment is to hold a tape measure up to the person you intend knitting for and decide how many inches or cms. wide you think you would like the picture to be. Translate the measurements into stitches and rows simply by checking the tension instructions in the knitting pattern you are going to use. This will give you the number of stitches and rows per inch or cm. For example, if it is 4 ply yarn you will be using with 7 stitches to the inch and you want the motif to be about 6 inches wide then the finished graph would need to be 6 x 7 stitches (= 42) squares wide. The same process is used for height and numbers of rows.
You must, of course, work out how many stitches and rows you have available on the garment panel you are going to work on. Your picture, when drawn on the graph paper, cannot take up more squares or stitches than will be available across the knitted piece, or more squares vertically than there are rows of knitting.

How to do Graphs

PREPARING THE DESIGN

The next step is to 'square up' the picture you are going to work from. It is not necessary to have an original drawing or picture the same size as the finished design. When translating the picture onto the graph paper you can scale it up as you require.

'Squaring up' means drawing a grid over the picture to act as a guide when you are copying onto the graph paper. I prefer to draw this grid onto tracing paper then lay it over my original picture so that I can use the same grid again and again. It also prevents damage to the original picture which may be of value.

The easiest way of deciding on the scale of the grid is to make the number of squares correspond to the number of inches you want the finished work to measure. In other words, if you are reproducing a portrait head and you want it to be 6 inches wide then divide the picture of the head into 6 squares across.

I usually start with the width as a first guide then draw the required number of squares vertically. You may of course draw a finer grid, but these adjustments are best made when you have a little experience of the technique.

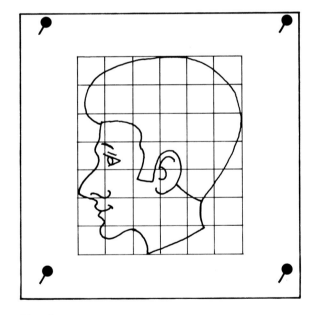

Fig. 1

TRANSFERRING THE DESIGN ONTO GRAPH PAPER

Now you have to draw a grid on the graph paper which corresponds with the grid over your picture. Again, you must take note of the knitting tension to be used. Each stitch will be represented by one square on the graph paper. Continuing with the 4 ply 'portrait' as the example, with 7 stitches to the inch, start marking out the six grid squares by counting along the bottom row 7 graph squares 6 times. This now forms the base and bottom line of the new, full scale grid on the graph paper.

The number of rows per inch in 4 ply is usually 9. Mark off vertically, therefore, as many sets of 9 graph squares as there are drawn squares on your original grid. In this way you will mark out on the graph paper a grid which corresponds to the grid over your picture but has different proportions. This second grid won't have exact squares but will be distorted to allow for the fact that on almost all knitting there are more rows to the inch than stitches. This is usually more noticeable on finer yarns and is particularly important to machine knitters where this sort of distortion can be extreme.

If you look at some of the ready drawn charts you will see that in order to get a circle on your garment, an elipse is drawn on the graph. This shows how the distortion takes place.

In many guides to motif knitting little is made of the distortion factor, but remember we are trying for really professional results here.

Next, lightly copy the picture under the first grid onto the grid on the graph paper. Do this one square at a time building up the picture slowly and accurately. Get the outline correct first

then fill in the details. As you will see, you don't need great skills in draughtsmanship since the grid keeps you right.

This grid technique serves a number of purposes: it scales up a source picture to the size you want; it keeps your drawing faithful to the original and at the same time adjusts the distortion factor in knitting from a picture. Artists and designers have always used this technique and even Michelangelo himself would have used it to scale up his sketches for the ceilings in the Sistine chapel. You will be in good company.

All that remains now is to go over the drawing more firmly with your pencil but this time follow the lines on your graph paper. Curves will be drawn in steps on the graph paper and the amount of detail will be determined by the number of squares at your disposal.

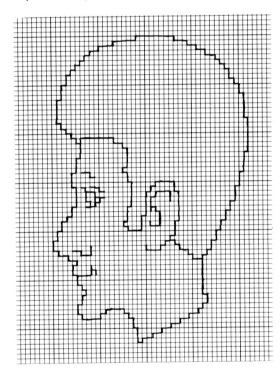

Fig. 3

Ignore very tiny details such as a single stitch to make a glint in an eye or very fine lines such as cat's whiskers. Make a note of where they go, but touches like this are best embroidered in afterwards.

Once you have completed the chart to your satisfaction colour the sections of your drawing with crayons. Don't cover your chart with those symbols for colours which appear on some knitting patterns as they are simply used by publishers to cut pattern printing costs. A coloured chart is much easier to look at and follow, so make yours a work of art.

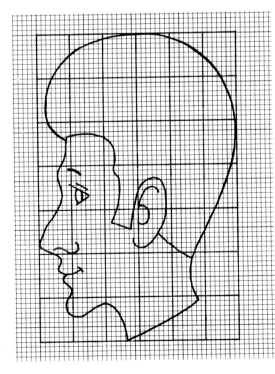

Fig. 2

How to use Graphs

You may not have knitted from a graph before, but don't worry, it's very straightforward and easy to follow. Each square on the graph paper represents one stitch of your knitting and you simply read across the graph row by row as you knit. If you are using one of the charts already printed in the book, remember to check that it is one which is suitable for the type of yarn you are using. They are drawn for 4 ply, double knitting and chunky, and are not really interchangeable.

To make a start you must decide on the position of the picture on the knitted garment. Do you want it in the centre? Do you want it to start down by the welt or halfway up the back? Do you want it on the sleeve? Once you have estimated roughly where it is to go, position it precisely by working out how many stitches wide your garment will be and how many rows there will be. Relate this information to the number of stitches (squares) your graph is and how many rows (squares) it will use vertically. In other words, if your picture is 50 stitches wide and the garment is 100 stitches wide you would knit 25 stitches each side of the picture area. Similarly, if there are 50 rows of knitting in the picture and 100 rows in the garment from welt to neck, then you would knit 25 rows below and above the picture. This example would place the picture in the centre of the knitting. If, for instance, you wanted to adjust this and have the picture a little higher, then you would knit more rows before the picture and fewer afterwards so long as the final number of rows knitted was still 100.

Hand Knitters

For hand knitters it is best to prepare the graph before starting by drawing, with a soft pencil, a box round the picture. The box should contain the pattern exactly. That means the box width is exactly the same width as the graph and the height exactly the height of the graph. By doing this you can see clearly the width and height of the motif. As you are knitting up the garment and reach the first row of the picture the drawn box simplifies the business of counting stitches and rows. Always start following the chart from the bottom right hand corner of the box. This first patterned row and every odd numbered row is worked from right to left. The even numbered rows are worked from left to right. Number the box carefully with your pencil either from 1 as the first row or by giving it the row number you have reached in your knitting.

Careful use of your row counter with the chart numberings will keep you right.

Machine Knitters

The instructions above can be used by machine knitters. However, since the needles on all machines are numbered out from the centre, you should mark and draw a line up through the centre of your chart. This is an invaluable guide for checking that you are following the pattern exactly as the knitting progresses. Mark the number of rows as the hand knitting instructions but get them to tally with the automatic row counter on your machine.

Some knitters may care to draw out the entire garment onto graph paper but unless you are tackling a very large scale picture which goes right round the body it really is not necessary.

Knitting Hints

HAND KNITTING HINTS

The designs in this book, although sometimes intricate in appearance are all based on very simple knitting techniques. The body panels are all knitted in stocking stitch – a stitch common to both hand and machine knitting. On the next few pages basic knitting hints and colour changing techniques will be clearly outlined.

HOW TO KNIT

First check your knitting kit, which should include, besides enthusiasm; ruler or tape measure, pins, stitch holders, row counter, knitting needle gauge and, of course, a selection of knitting needles.

CASTING ON
Fig 1. Casting on provides the first row of loops on your needle. There are several methods of doing this but the easiest is as follows. You need two knitting needles. Make a slip loop in the end of the ball of yarn and put it on the left hand needle. Holding the yarn in the right hand insert the right hand needle into the loop, wind the yarn under and over the right hand needle and draw a loop through the slip loop. Put the newly made stitch onto the left hand needle. This makes one stitch. Continue like this working into the last stitch made on the left hand needle each time until you have the number of stitches required by the pattern.

STOCKING STITCH
Stocking stitch is formed by alternate rows of knitting and purling and its appearance is that of 'plain' knitting.

Fig 1.
Casting on

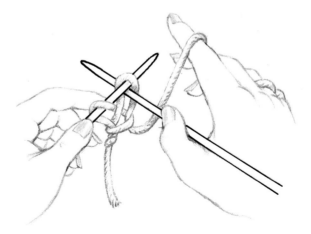

KNITTING
Fig 2. Hold the needle with the cast on stitches in your left hand and the other needle and yarn in your right hand. Insert the right hand needle into the front of the first loop on the left hand needle. Keeping the yarn at the back of the work pass it under and over the top of the right hand needle and draw a loop through the stitch on the left hand needle.

Fig 2.
Knitting – to begin stitch

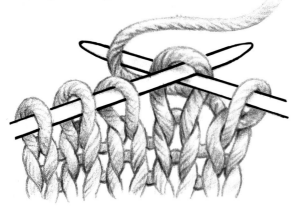

Fig 3.
Knitting – to complete stitch

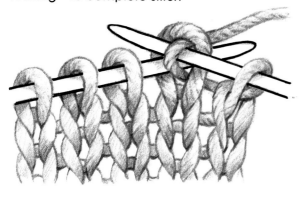

Fig 3. Keep this new stitch on the right hand needle and let the stitch on the left hand needle slip off. Continue in this way until all the stitches are transferred to the right hand needle. Transfer the right hand needle holding the stitches to your left hand, turn the work round and start the next row.

Fig 4.
Purling – to begin stitch

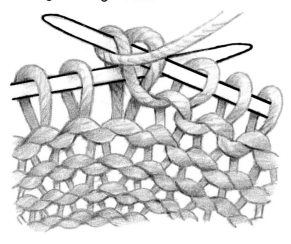

PURLING
Figs 4 & 5. Hold the needle with the cast on stitches in your left hand with the yarn and the other needle in your right hand.

Insert the right hand needle into the front of the first stitch from right to left, keeping the yarn at the front of the work wind the yarn round the top of the right hand needle and draw a loop through the stitch on the left hand needle.

Fig 5.
Purling – to complete stitch

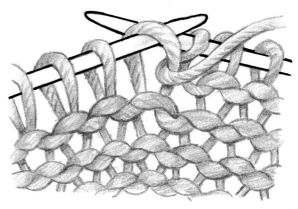

Keep this new stitch on the right hand needle and let the stitch on the left hand needle slip off. Continue in this way until all the stitches are transferred to the right hand needle. Transfer the right hand needle to your left hand, turning the work around. You are ready to start the next row.

Fig 6.
Casting off

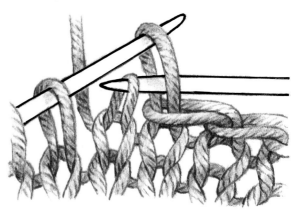

CASTING OFF
Fig 6. Knit the first two stitches of the row leaving them on the right hand needle. With the point of the left hand needle lift the first stitch over the second stitch and slip it off the needle, leaving only one stitch on the right hand needle. Knit another stitch making two stitches on the right hand needle again. Repeat the process of lifting the first stitch over the second and slipping it off the needle and continue until the required number of stitches have been cast off. Cut the yarn, allowing yourself a short length to pass through the last stitch and fasten off.

SINGLE RIB
This is the most common of all knitted stitches used to form an elastic texture for welts, cuffs and neckbands.
Single rib is made by knitting the first stitch of the first row, bringing the yarn forward to the front of the work, purling the next stitch and taking the yarn back between the needles again ready for the next stitch. Continue in this way until all the stitches are transferred to the right hand needle. On the next row, the stitches which were knitted on the first row are purled and the stitches which were purled are knitted.

A double rib is sometimes used and this is simply a variation of the instructions already given but based on a combination of knit two, purl two.

JOINING YARN
It is always best to join in a new ball of yarn at the beginning of a new row. A knot in the middle of a row can produce very unsatisfactory results.

TENSION
Once you have mastered the basic techniques of knitting, the next step is to understand the importance of achieving the correct tension. Without a little care taken over this initial task, hours of knitting can be wasted.
Tension simply means the number of stitches and rows to a particular given measurement. Since every knitting pattern is based on a particular ratio of these it is essential to check your tension before beginning a pattern.
Three things determine the tension of your knitted fabric; size of needles, thickness of yarn and personal knitting technique. The first two are always recommended in any pattern but even with this information it is essential to check. There are tremendous variations in thickness between yarns of the same 'ply' from different spinners. For instance, the classic patterns in this book recommend standard yarns and give an average tension for that 'ply' yarn. You may find however, that having purchased the correct yarn and using the recommended needles the tension is not exactly right. Adjustments can be made as outlined below.

HOW TO CHECK THE TENSION
Knit a small square measuring at least 10cm. (4in.) using the recommended yarn and size of needles. Lay this sample on a flat surface and using a firm ruler mark out 5cm. (2ins.), (or the measurement recommended in the pattern) across stitches and rows. Mark this square with pins.

If there are more rows or stitches in the pinned area than the given tension measurement then you need to change to bigger needles. If there are too few stitches or rows, then use smaller needles.

Fig 7.
Tension

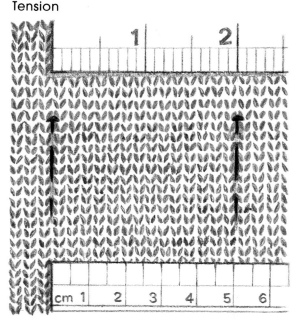

Fig 7. The importance of checking tension cannot be overstressed. A variation from that suggested in the pattern can result in a garment wildly too big or far too small. If you should find, with the yarn you have, that the correct width and depth of tension is impossible to obtain settle for the correct number of stitches. The depth of the knitting can always be adjusted by working more or less rows as required.

COLOUR AND YARN CHANGING TECHNIQUES
The patterns described in the book are meant to encourage those knitters who are interested in 'picture' knitting, which of course requires learning the techniques of changing from one colour or yarn to another. These basic skills are simple to learn and once mastered allow you to keep your knitting smooth and neat, no matter how intricate the design you are following.

To change to a new yarn at the start of a row, as in striping etc, tie a knot with the new yarn in the last loop of the row below the one just completed. Leave a reasonable end of free yarn so that it can be darned out of sight when the garment panel is finished.

Changing yarn or colour in the middle of a row can be achieved in a number of ways. Outlined next is the easiest method of producing a really smooth transition.

Fig 8.
Introducing a new colour in the middle of a row

Fig 9.
The first stitch in a new colour

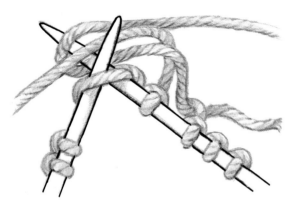

Fig 10.
Using the new colour

Figs 8, 9 & 10. Knit or purl to one stitch before the position where the change of yarn is to begin and put the right needle into the stitch, lay the new yarn over the point of the needle, leaving a long enough end to darn in later, and work the stitch. Put the point of the right hand needle into the next stitch. Take the first yarn over the top of the right hand needle and, while holding it there, knit or purl with the new yarn.
Work the second stitch with the new yarn which will cross the original yarn at the back and hold it securely. Carry on knitting with the new yarn.

STRANDING, WEAVING AND CROSSING YARNS OR COLOURS

When knitting with more than one yarn or colour in any one row you must make a decision between carrying the yarns along the entire row or changing from one yarn to another leaving each to be picked up on the next row. The decision you make will depend on how many stitches a contrast yarn would have to be carried across. For only two or three stitches the stranding method is best. If there are more than this the contrast yarn must be woven in to avoid long loops or floats of yarn forming at the back of the work. For large blocks of yarn change, separate balls of yarn should be used for each section, crossing the colours at the join.

Fig 11.
Stranding in a knit row

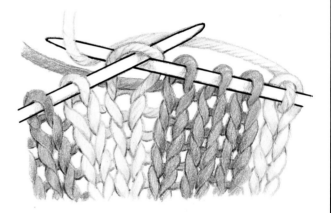

STRANDING

Figs 11 & 12. Stranding simply means carrying the contrast yarn not in use loosely across the work until it is needed. When stranding in a knit row the loose yarn is always at the back of the work. Check that the two yarns have crossed at the back when changing to avoid a hole appearing between the contrasting stitches.

Fig 12.
Stranding in a purl row

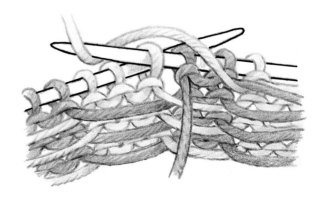

Stranding on a purl row is the same as on a knit row but the yarns are loosely stranded across the front of the work. Take care not to pull the stranded yarns too tightly so that the appearance of the knitting is flat and even and not puckered or too tightly tensioned.

Fig 13.
Weaving in a knit row

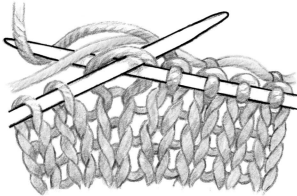

Fig 14.
Weaving in a purl row

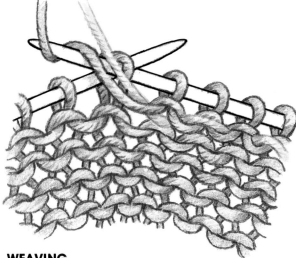

WEAVING

Figs 13 & 14. Weaving is the technique used to 'catch up' a contrast yarn across the back of the knitting until needed. When weaving in a knit row carry the contrast yarn behind the work over your left index finger. Push the point of the right hand needle under the contrast yarn and knit the stitch. Knit the next stitch as normal. In this way the contrast yarn is secured behind the main work. This can be done about every three or four stitches, or every other stitch.

When weaving in a purl row carry the contrast yarn in front of the work over your left index finger. Push the point of the right hand needle purlwise into the next stitch. Bring the contrast yarn in front of both needles and purl the stitch. Purl the next stich as normal.

Again, as with stranding, take care not to pull the contrast yarns too tightly.

Fig 15.
Crossing colours in a knit row

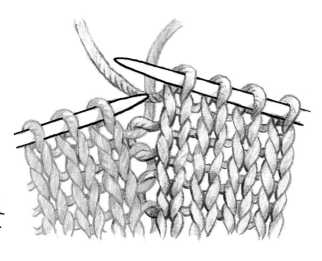

Fig 16.
Crossing colours in a purl row

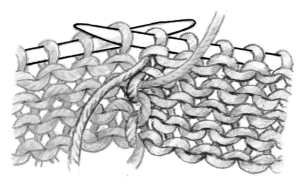

CROSSING YARNS

Figs 15 & 16. When knitting large blocks of contrast colour, separate balls of yarn should be used, crossing them when a join is reached to avoid holes forming. The contrast yarns are not carried across the back of the work but are left to be picked up on the returning row.

You will need to wind a small ball of each contrasting yarn needed in any one row. The size of the ball will be determined by the number of stitches and rows that any particular block of contrast requires. Start each new ball as required leaving enough yarn for darning in later. When moving from one yarn to another they must be crossed where they join.

When crossing yarns in a knit row insert the right hand needle into the first stitch of the contrast yarn before crossing the first yarn over the second (contrast) at the back of the work. Then continue knitting with the second yarn. Knit the first stitch of the contrast yarn firmly to form a neat join. When crossing yarns in a purl row insert the right hand needle into the first stitch of the contrast yarn before crossing the first yarn under the second (contrast) at the front of the work. Again, the first purl stitch should be firmly made for a neat join.

When making your decision about which technique to use when changing colours and yarns remember that any garment can contain all three depending upon the design and its complexity.

DARNING IN THE ENDS
In the yarn changing techniques described, reference is made to leaving ends of yarn at joins to be darned in later. It is well worth spending time on this to make a firm join between one yarn and another and to give the finished garment a neat, flat appearance. Avoid simple knotting as far as possible, particularly when using thicker yarns.

Fig 17.
Swiss darning

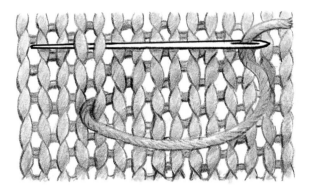

SWISS DARNING
Fig 17. Swiss darning is a very useful form of embroidery in which you cover the original knitted stitch with another colour or yarn. It is especially useful in 'picture' knitting and can be used to fill in small design details which would be fiddly to knit. It is, for that matter, useful in correcting small mistakes which you might spot after completing a whole section.
The best results are obtained using a yarn the same thickness as the original knitting threaded through a blunt wool needle.
When done neatly swiss darning is virtually indistinguishable from the original knitting. It is a simple technique best described by following the given diagram.

FINISHING AND SEWING UP

PRESSING
Follow the instructions given with the yarn. Some yarns must barely be touched while others benefit from a good steaming. Pin or lay out each piece of knitting with the wrong side uppermost. With a steam iron carefully coax each piece into its correct shape and see that it is nicely flat. **Don't** under any circumstances, press the iron heavily onto the knitting and **don't** treat knitwear as though it were a damp shirt.

If you don't have a steam iron use a damp cloth and an ordinary iron.

SEWING UP
Bear in mind the hours you have put into the garment when you approach this final stage. Careless sewing up can so easily spoil a beautifully knitted garment.

Fig 18.
Invisible seam

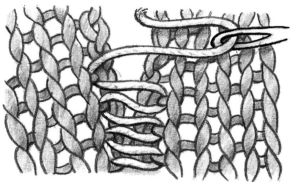

Fig 18. Use an invisible seam for the side and sleeve seams. It is quite possible to sew two pieces together so that the join can barely be spotted.
The technique is to sew with the right sides of the knitted pieces facing you. Place the two edges to be joined close together and begin by securing the yarn at one end bringing the needle and yarn to the right side of the work. Take the needle across and insert it under the bar which connects the first and second stitch of the row. Draw the needle through and insert it through the corresponding bar on the other piece of knitting.
Continue weaving across the two pieces drawing them together as you go along.

Fig 19.
Backstitch seaming

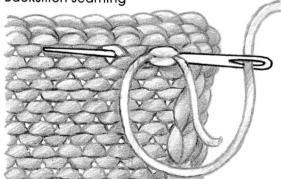

Fig 19. Backstitch when the seam to be made runs across the direction of the knitting, as in the shoulder seam. Place the two edges, right sides together and secure the yarn at the right hand edge of the work. Backstitch the seam from right to left moving one stitch to the right at the front and two stitches to the left at the back.

YARNS

Success with your finished garment depends not only on your knitting abilities, but to a large extent on your initial choice of yarn.

No specific yarns have been recommended in this book and although the illustrated garments show particular colours these are only suggestions. Final decisions should be made by yourself and will depend both on the idea you have in mind and what colours and textures are available to you in your local knitting shop. I have found from experience that wide ranges of texture and quality can be obtained easily from retail outlets whereas mail order companies seem to offer yarns in a wide range of colours. So do shop around to see what's available before making a final decision.

I make one or two comments about yarn thicknesses in the Basic Classics section. If you refer to these you will see that I encourage any knitter not to be afraid to substitute yarns. Provided you get the tension of your knitting to match the pattern you are guaranteed success.

There does seem to be some confusion about qualities of yarn. The old idea that wool is best and synthetics are nasty no longer holds true. Vast ranges of exciting yarns are found on display in any knitting shop and these can be based on natural or manmade fibres or more likely a mixture of both.

Wool
Pure wool is, in the main, slightly more expensive than equivalent synthetic yarns. It does, however, tend to keep its shape and behave more predictably than synthetics. Care in washing is necessary but it can be very long lasting particularly when mixed with nylon. It is excellent for motif work, as the yarn 'stays together' and changes from one colour to another can be made neatly. This is not always the case with more slippery synthetic yarns.

Synthetic Yarns
There is a much wider range of colour and texture to be found in synthetic yarns. 'Fancy Yarns' are almost all based upon synthetics and many familiar names like angora and mohair now have cheaper synthetic equivalents. The fluffier synthetic yarns are again excellent for picture or motif knitting but care should be taken in the finishing and pressing stages. These yarns are easily stretched or flattened by insensitive handling.

Cotton and Silk
These yarns are not recommended for motif work as they tend to be slippery and difficult to use in any colour changing technique. Small quantities can be used for details but generally speaking leave these yarns for more straightforward classic knits.

Metallics
'Metallic' yarns give the impression of being made of thin strips or threads of real metal but they are, like sequins, made of plastic. They can be bought under a variety of trade names and are wonderful for flashy detail work. You will find that ranges of metallic threads are now available and these can be used in conjunction with plain yarns to produce your own fancy effects.

Yarn Quantities
The amount of yarn needed for your garment will be shown on the pattern you use. If you intend building the pattern using a greater variety of colours you must calculate roughly how much of the garment will be knitted with each yarn.

This should be straightforward enough but be prepared to err on the generous side for each colour. There will, unavoidably, be rather more wastage when using lots of colours and yarns. Also remember when substituting yarns that synthetics weigh less than natural yarns and since yarn is sold by weight a 50 gram ball of synthetic yarn will go further than a 50 gram ball of wool. The knitting shop where you buy your yarn should be able to advise you on length of yarn in a ball.

In picture knitting there will be occasions when only tiny quantities of one colour will be required. When that occurs have a good root around in your knitting bag for odds and ends. Don't be afraid to substitute different yarns or double them up to get the right thickness, as any change will hardly be noticed on a small area.

However, the one thing to remember is not to mix pure synthetics with natural yarns as they act differently when being washed and pressed. Having said that, do try out yarns of varying texture.

Machine Knitting

Knitting need no longer be the time consuming craft of yesteryear. The speed, flexibility and accuracy of knitting by machine has created a huge growth in the popularity of the craft. In fact many machine knitters manage perfectly well without ever having knitted a single stitch by hand.

I won't attempt to delve into the basics of machine knitting. Although the knitting which is produced by one machine is much the same as that produced by another the techniques usually differ slightly and are amply covered in instruction manuals. It may be however, that you have not attempted 'picture' knitting or intarsia work with your machine before and one or two pieces of advice would be helpful.

Most machines are designed to knit two colour, fairisle, repeat patterns. This is fine, as far as it goes, and is ideal for quick patterning. Some punchcard machines can be made to knit single motifs but these are usually limited to no more than 24 stitches wide which is quite a narrow area. In the case of non punchcard machines or with the use of an intarsia carriage on a punchcard type it is possible however, to knit several colours or yarns in one row and over any number of needles.

INTARSIA

This process is one which accommodates hand selection of the needles for your pattern and usually means that the various yarns are laid across the needles rather than coming through the yarn feeder.
Each yarn knits back and forth within its own designed shape rather than looping or floating at the back of the work as in fairisle.
The machine is set up as if to knit repeat fairisle with all the required needles brought forward to the position for knitting the pattern colour or yarn.
A length or ball of yarn is usually required for each separate area of colour or texture. Always lay the yarn across the needles starting from the side nearest the carriage. Lay an end of yarn in the appropriate colour or texture across each group of needles determined by the design. Each new yarn should overlap the last by one needle so that the stitches are held together and a hole does not form between colours on the finished work. Pass the carriage across the machine once all the needles have been covered and bring the needles back to the knitting position. You are now ready to start the next row laying the yarns back across the machine in the other direction.

Don't forget that in machine knitting, unlike hand knitting, the back of the work always faces you. This means that when following a graph straight the picture will be reversed on your garment. This may not matter, but if you are following a design using words, letters or something similar you must work the design backwards. The technique is not as difficult as it sounds and simply requires you to count the squares of the graph one way and count the correct number of needles in the other direction on the machine.

It is probably worth noting that on some machines the fairisle technique allows you to select pattern needles by hand and lay in pattern yarn while knitting with the main yarn through the yarn feeder. This will produce floats on the back of the work but is very quick and is ideal for designs which use small groups of needles.

There are of course, very sophisticated machines now appearing for the home knitter which will produce large motifs automatically. These are however, relatively expensive and to my mind do not produce patterning of the quality which a careful knitter can expect from a more basic model.

Basic Classics

In this section you will find detailed knitting instructions for the seven classic styles which were chosen for the illustrations in the book. Each garment is straightforward to knit with a minimum of shaping, so that you can concentrate on getting your 'picture knitting' techniques perfected.

There are two cardigans shown, one a 4 ply classic, the other a 50's styled, chunky, outdoor garment. The two slipovers are meant to contrast, one a youthful, boxy, vest style, the other a classic V neck. The three sweaters are all basic shapes with differing collar detail and each in a different thickness of yarn. All the garments are quite suitable for both sexes and can be made to look conservative, wild, sporty, chic or whatever, by interpreting them as you like with different designs, pictures and colours.

The yarns recommended are described simply as Chunky, Double Knit or 4 ply. You can of course use any yarn which will approximate the tensions given in the patterns. Modern yarn manufacturers are less inclined to give their products 'ply' references than they did at one time – rather exotic names have been substituted. So don't be shy about experimenting with yarns. All good 'Wool' shops are only too happy to give you advice on suitable equivalent yarns.

CLASSIC 4-PLY SWEATER.

MATERIALS
Yarn (for plain sweater)
10 (10 : 11 : 12 : 12) x 50g balls 4-ply.

Needles
1 pair 2¾mm (UK 12)
1 pair 3¼mm (UK 10)

MEASUREMENTS
Bust/Chest
86 (91 : 97 : 102 : 107)cm
34 (36 : 38 : 40 : 42)in

Actual Size
91 (94 : 100 : 106 : 109)cm
36 (37 : 39 : 41¾ : 42¾)in

Length
62 (66 : 68 : 70 : 71)cm
24½ (26 : 27 : 27½ : 28)in

Sleeve Seam
48cm (19in)

TENSION
14 sts and 18 rows = 5cm (2in) square
on 3¼mm needles (UK 10) (or size needed
to obtain given tension).

BACK
With 2¾mm needles cast on 128 (132 :
140 : 148 : 152) sts. Work in K2, P2 rib for
7cm (2¾in).
Change to 3¼mm needles, and starting
with a K row, work in st. st. Cont. straight
until work measures 38 (42 : 44 : 46 : 47)cm
15 (16½ : 17½ : 18 : 18½)in from beg.
ending with a P row.

Shape Armholes
Dec. 1 st. at both ends on next 8 rows.
(112 (116 : 124 : 132 : 136) sts.). Work
straight until armhole measures 24cm
(9½in), ending with a P row.

Shape Shoulders
Cast off 7 (7 : 7 : 8 : 8) sts. at beg. of next
8 rows, and 4 (5 : 8 : 8 : 9) sts. at beg. of
next 2 rows.
Leave rem. 48 (50 : 52 : 52 : 54) sts. on a
holder.

FRONT
Work as for back until armhole measures
16cm (6½in).

Shape Neck
With R.S. of work facing K44 (45 : 48 : 52 :
53) sts., turn, leave rem. sts. on a spare
needle.
*Dec. 1 st. at neck edge on the next
12 rows. Work straight until length
measures same as back to shoulder,
ending at armhole edge.

Shape Shoulder
Cast off 7 (7 : 7 : 8 : 8) sts. at beg. of next
and foll. 3 alt. rows. Work 1 row. Cast off 4
(5 : 8 : 8 : 9) sts.
With R.S. facing, slip next 24 (26 : 28 : 28 :
30) sts. on to a holder. Rejoin yarn to next
st. and K to end of row. Complete to
match first side from * to end.

SLEEVES
With 2¾mm needles cast on 68 sts. Work in
K2, P2 rib for 8cm (3¼in). On the last row
inc. 16 sts. evenly along row (84 sts.).
Change to 3¼mm needles, and starting
with a K row, work in st. st. inc. 1 st. at both
ends of every foll. 5th row until there are
132 sts. Work straight until sleeve measures
48cm (19in), or desired length, from beg.
ending with a P row.

Shape Top
Dec. 1 st. at both ends of next 8 rows.
(116 sts.). Cast off.

NECKBAND
Sew up left shoulder seam.
With 2¾mm needles and R.S. work facing,
pick up and K48 (50 : 52 : 52 : 54) sts. from
back neck, 24 sts. from left side neck,
24 (26 : 28 : 28 : 30) sts. from centre front,
and 24 sts. from right side neck. (120 (124 :
128 : 128 : 132) sts.). Work in K2, P2 rib for
5cm (2in). Cast off loosely in rib.

TO MAKE UP
Press work according to yarn instructions,
omitting ribbing.
Sew up right shoulder and neckband.
Fold neckband in half and sew down
on W.S.
Sew in sleeves. Sew up side and
sleeve seams.

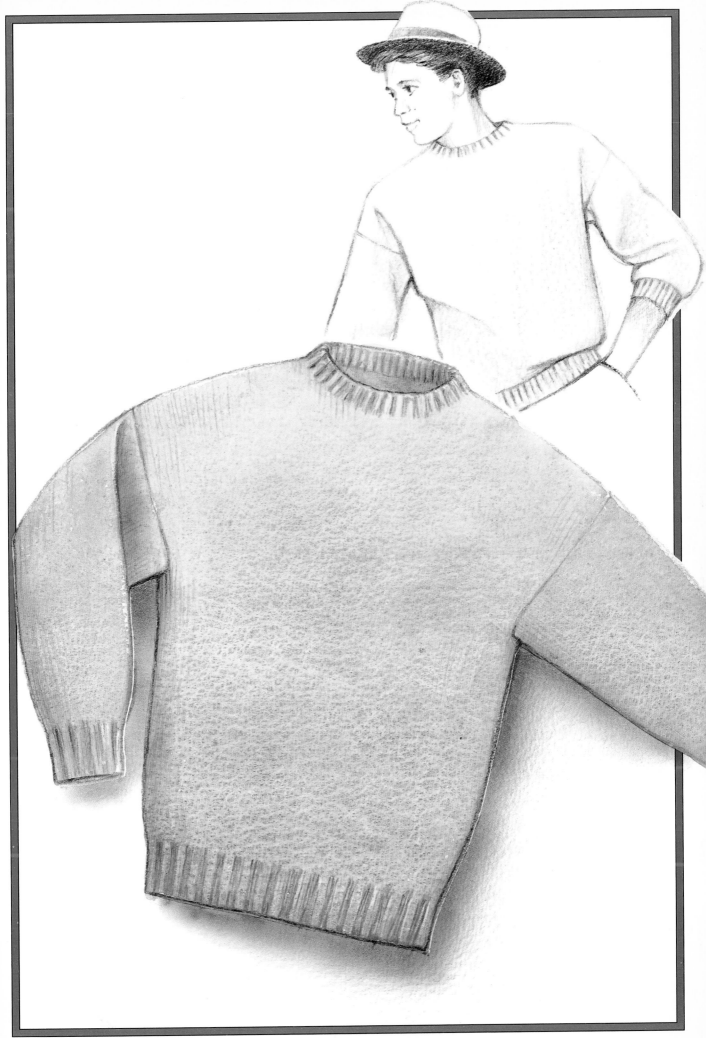

'V' NECK SLIPOVER IN DOUBLE KNIT.

MATERIALS

Yarn (for plain slipover)
9 (10 : 12 : 14) x 50g balls D.K.

Needles
1 pair 3mm (UK 11)
1 pair 3¾mm (UK 9)

MEASUREMENTS

Bust/Chest
86/91 (97/102 : 107/112 : 117)cm
34/36 (38/40 : 42/44 : 46)in

Actual Size
102 (112 : 120 : 129)cm
40 (44 : 47 : 51)in

Length
61 (62 : 64 : 65)cm
24 (24½ : 25 : 25½)in

TENSION

22 sts. and 30 rows = 10cm (4in) square on
3¾mm needles (UK 9) (or size needed to
obtain given tension).

BACK

Cast on 112 (122 : 132 : 142) sts. with 3mm
needles. Work in K1, P1 rib for 6cm (2¼in).
Change to 3¾mm needles and starting
with a K row, work in st. st.
Cont. straight until work measures 37cm
(14½in) from beg. ending with a P row.

Shape Armholes
Cast off 3 (3 : 4 : 5) sts. at beg. next 2 rows.
Cast off 2 (3 : 3 : 4) sts. at beg. next 2 rows.
Cast off 2 (2 : 2 : 3) sts. at beg. next 2 rows.*
Cast off 2 sts. at beg. next 2 (2 : 4 : 4) rows.
Cast off 1 st. at beg. next 4 (6 : 4 : 4) rows.
(90 (96 : 102 : 106) sts.).
Cont. straight until work measures
61 (62 : 64 : 65)cm, 24 (24½ : 25 : 25½)in
from beg. ending with a P row.

Shape Shoulders and Neck
Cast off 5 (5 : 6 : 6) sts. at beg. next 4 rows.
Next row – Cast off 6 sts., K24 (26 : 26 : 27)
sts., cast off 10 (12 : 14 : 16) sts. K to end.
Work each side of neck separately.
Next row – Cast off 6 sts. P to end.
Next row – Cast off 7 sts. at neck edge,
K to end.
Next row – Cast off 6 sts. P to end.
Next row – Cast off 7 sts. at neck edge,
K to end.
Next row – Cast off rem. 4 (6 : 6 : 7) sts.
Rejoin yarn at neck edge and complete
other side of neck to match, reversing
shaping.

FRONT

Work as for back to *.

Divide for Neck
Cast off 2 (2 : 2 : 2) sts., K47 (51 : 55 : 57) sts.,
turn and leave rem. 49 (53 : 57 : 59) sts. on a
spare needle.
Work each side of neck separately.
Next row – P2 tog., P to end.
Next row – Cast off 1 (1 : 2 : 2) sts., K to end.
Next row – P.
Next row – Cast off 1 (1 : 1 : 1) st., K to last
2 sts. K2 tog.
Cast off 1 st. at armhole edge on alt. row 0
(1 : 1 : 1) time more and cont. to dec.
1 st. at neck edge every foll. 3rd row
17 (18 : 19 : 20) times more.
When work measures same as back to
shoulder ending at armhole edge,

Shape Shoulder
Cast off 5 (5 : 6 : 6) sts. at beg. of next and
foll. alt. rows 2 (2 : 5 : 4) times in all.
Cast off 6 (6 : 0 : 7) sts. at beg. of alt. rows 2
(3 : 0 : 1) times.
First size only
Work 1 row. Cast off rem. 4 sts.

Rejoin yarn at neck edge and complete to
match other side of neck reversing
shaping.

ARMHOLE BANDS (make 2)

With 3mm needles cast on 130 (138 : 148 :
154) sts. Work 2.5cm (1in) in K1, P1 rib. Knit 1
row. Cast off.

NECKBAND

With 3mm needles cast on 136 (144 : 152 :
160) sts.
1st row – *, K1, P1, rep. from * to end.
2nd row – (W.S.) Rib 67 (71 : 75 : 79) sts.,
Make 1 (pick up bar between next st.,
place on left needle and work into back of
loop to inc. 1 st.), P1 (mark st. with col.
thread), Make 1, rib to end.
Inc. 1 st. each side of marked st. on next 6
rows. K 1 row. Cast off.

TO MAKE UP

Press work according to yarn instructions,
omitting ribbing. Join shoulder and side
seams. Join armhole bands and neckband
and sew in place.

CLASSIC SWEATER WITH OPTIONAL COLLAR IN DOUBLE KNIT.

MATERIALS

Yarn (for plain sweater)
10 (12 : 12 : 14 : 14 : 16) x 50g balls D.K.

Needles
1 pair 3¾mm (UK 9)
1 pair 4mm (UK 8)

MEASUREMENTS

Bust/Chest
86 (91 : 97 : 102 : 107 : 112)cm
34 (36 : 38 : 40 : 42 : 44)in

Actual Size
95 (100 : 105 : 110 : 117 : 122)cm
37½ (39 : 41½ : 43 : 46 : 48)in

Length
63 (64 : 66 : 67 : 70 : 71)cm
24¾ (25 : 26 : 26½ : 27½ : 28)in

Sleeve Length
49cm (19¼in)

TENSION
22 sts. and 28 rows = 10cm (4in) square on 4mm needles (UK 8) (or size needed to obtain given tension).

BACK
Cast on 104 (110 : 116 : 122 : 128 : 134) sts. with 3¾mm needles. Work in K1 P1 rib for 7.5cm (3in).
Change to 4mm needles and starting with a K row, work in st. st. Cont. straight until work measures 36 (36 : 37 : 37 : 38 : 38)cm 14 (14 : 14½ : 14½ : 15 : 15)in from beg. Mark each end of last row with a col. thread for beg. of armhole.
Cont. straight until armhole measures 27 (28 : 29 : 30 : 32 : 33)cm, 10½ (11 : 11½ : 12 : 12½ : 13)in ending with a P row.

Shape Shoulders
Cast off 9 (10 : 11 : 11 : 12 : 13) sts. at beg. of next 4 rows, and 10 (11 : 11 : 13 : 14 : 14) sts. at beg. of next 2 rows.
Leave rem. 48 (48 : 50 : 52 : 52 : 54) sts. on a holder.

FRONT
Work as for back until armhole measures 18 rows less than back to shoulder, ending with a P row.

Shape Neck
Next row – K42 (45 : 47 : 50 : 52 : 55) sts., turn, leave rem. sts. on a spare needle.
* Dec. 1 st. at neck edge on next 14 (14 : 14 : 15 : 14 : 15) rows. (28 (31 : 33 : 35 : 38 : 40) sts.). Work straight until armhole measures same as back to shoulder, ending at armhole edge.

Shape Shoulder
Cast off 9 (10 : 11 : 11 : 12 : 13) sts. at beg. of next and foll. alt. row. Work 1 row. Cast off 10 (11 : 11 : 13 : 14 : 14) sts.
With R.S. facing sl. the next 20 (20 : 22 : 22 : 24 : 24) sts. onto a holder. Rejoin yarn to next st. and K to end of row. Complete to match first side from * to end.

SLEEVES
Cast on 60 (62 : 64 : 66 : 68 : 70) sts. with 3¾mm needles. Work in K1, P1 rib for 15cm (6in). On the last row inc. 10 (12 : 12 : 14 : 14 : 16) sts. evenly along the row. (70 (74 : 76 : 80 : 82 : 86) sts.).
Change to 4mm needles and starting with a K row, work in st. st. **At the same time** inc. 1 st. at each end of every 3rd. row until there are 118 (122 : 128 : 134 : 140 : 146) sts. Cont. straight until work measures 49cm (19¼in) or required length from beg. Cast off loosely.

COLLAR
Cast on 118 (118 : 122 : 124 : 126 : 128) sts. loosely with 3¾mm needles. Work in K1, P1 rib for 7.5cm (3in). Cast off loosely in rib.

NECKBAND
Sew up left shoulder seam.
With R.S. facing and 3¾mm needles, pick up and K48 (48 : 50 : 52 : 52 : 54) sts. from back neck, 18 sts. from left side neck, 20 (20 : 22 : 22 : 24 : 24) sts. from centre front and 18 sts. from right side neck. (104 (104 : 108 : 110 : 112 : 114) sts.). Work in K1, P1 rib for 2.5cm (1in). Cast off loosely in rib.

MAKING UP
Press work according to yarn instructions omitting ribbing. Sew up right shoulder and neckband seam. Mark centre of front neck. Sew cast-on edge of collar around inside of neckband, with side edges of collar meeting at centre front. Fold collar to outside. Sew top of sleeves to back and front between markers. Sew up side and sleeve seams.

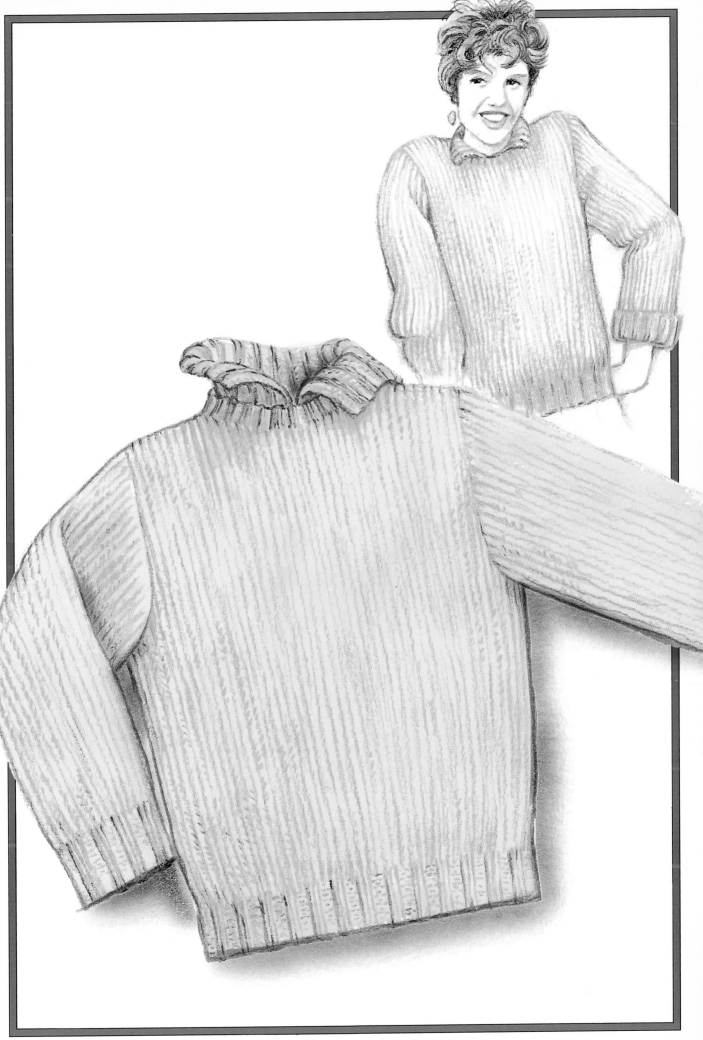

CHUNKY SWEATER.

MATERIALS
Yarn 11 (12 : 13 : 14 : 14 : 15) x 10g balls chunky yarn.

Needles
1 pair 4½mm (UK 7)
1 pair 6mm (UK 4)

MEASUREMENTS

Bust/Chest
86 (91 : 97 : 102 : 107 : 112)cm
34 (36 : 38 : 40 : 42 : 44)in

Actual Size
97 (102 : 107 : 112 : 117 : 122)cm
38 (40 : 42 : 44 : 46 : 48)in

Length
60 (61 : 62 : 64 : 65 : 66)cm
23½ (24 : 24½ : 25 : 25½ : 26)in

Sleeve Seam
40 (41 : 41 : 41 : 42 : 43)cm
15½ (16 : 16 : 16 : 16½ : 17)in

TENSION
15 sts and 20 rows = 10cm (4in) square on 6mm needles (UK 4) (or size needed to obtain given tension).

BACK
*With 4½mm needles cast on 63 (67 : 71 : 75 : 79 : 83) sts. and work in K1, P1 rib for 7cm (2¾in) beg. W.S. rows P1.. On the last row inc. 9 sts. evenly. (72 (76 : 80 : 84 : 88 : 92) sts.).
Change to 6mm needles and starting with a K row, work in st. st. Cont. straight until work measures 35cm (13¾in) from beg. ending with a P row.

Shape Raglans
Cast off 2 sts. at beg. of next 2 rows.
First, second and fourth sizes: Dec. 1 st. at both ends of next row. Work 3 rows. (66 (70 : 78) sts.).*
All sizes: Dec. 1 st. at both ends of next and every alt. row until 22 (24 : 24 : 26 : 26 : 28) sts. rem. Work 1 row. Cast off.

FRONT
Work as for Back from * to *.
All sizes: Dec 1 st. at both ends of next and every alt. row until 34 (36 : 36 : 40 : 40 : 42) sts. rem., ending with a P row.

Shape Neck
Next row – K2 tog., K10 (10 : 10 : 11 : 11 : 11) sts., turn and leave rem. sts. on a spare needle.** Dec. 1 st. at neck edge on next 4 rows, **at the same time** cont. to dec. 1 st. at raglan edge on every alt. row until 2 sts. rem. K2 tog.
With R.S. facing rejoin yarn to rem. sts. and cast off centre 10 (12 : 12 : 14 : 14 : 16) sts. K to last 2 sts., K2 tog.
Complete to match first side from ** to end.

SLEEVES
With 4½mm needles cast on 27 (29 : 31 : 31 : 33 : 33) sts. and work in K1, P1 rib as for back for 6cm (2¼in). On the last row inc. 7 sts. evenly (34 (36 : 38 : 38 : 40 : 40) sts.).
Change to 6mm needles and starting with a K row, work in st. st. Inc. 1 st. at both ends of 7th and every foll. 4th row until there are 60 (62 : 64 : 66 : 68 : 70) sts. Work straight until sleeve measures 40 (41 : 41 : 41 : 42 : 43)cm, 15½ (16 : 16 : 16 : 16½ : 17)in, or required length, from beg. ending with a P row.

Shape Raglans
Cast off 2 sts. at beg. of next 2 rows. Dec. 1 st. at both ends of next and every alt. row until 10 (10 : 10 : 6 : 6 : 6) sts. rem.
Work 1 row.
First, second and third sizes: Dec. 1 st. at both ends of next 2 rows.
All sizes: Cast off rem. 6 sts.

COLLAR
With 4½mm needles cast on 81 (87 : 103 : 103 : 111 : 111) sts. and work 7 rows in K1, P1 rib as for back.
8th row – Rib 69 (75 : 91 : 91 : 99 : 99) sts., turn.
9th row – Sl. 1, rib 56 (62 : 78 : 78 : 86 : 86) sts., turn.
10th row – Sl. 1, rib 58 (64 : 80 : 80 : 88 : 88) sts., turn.
11th row – Sl. 1, rib 60 (66 : 82 : 82 : 90 : 90) sts., turn.
12th row – Sl. 1, rib 62 (68 : 84 : 84 : 92 : 92) sts., turn.
13th row – Sl. 1, rib 64 (70 : 86 : 86 : 94 : 94) sts., turn.
14th row – Sl. 1, rib 66 (72 : 88 : 88 : 96 : 96) sts., turn.
15th row – Sl. 1, rib 68 (74 : 90 : 90 : 98 : 98) sts., turn.
16th row – Sl. 1, rib 66 (72 : 88 : 88 : 96 : 96) sts., turn.
17th row – Sl. 1, rib 64 (70 : 86 : 86 : 94 : 94) sts., turn.
18th row – Sl. 1, rib 62 (68 : 84 : 84 : 92 : 92) sts., turn.
19th row – Sl. 1, rib 60 (66 : 82 : 82 : 90 : 90) sts., turn.
20th row – Sl. 1, rib 58 (64 : 80 : 80 : 88 : 88) sts., turn.
21st row – Sl. 1, rib 56 (62 : 78 : 78 : 86 : 86) sts., turn.
22nd row – Sl. 1, rib to end.
Work 7 more rows in rib. Cast off loosely in rib.

TO MAKE UP
Press work according to yarn instructions omitting ribbing.
Join raglan, side and sleeve seams.
Sew cast off and side edges of collar in position evenly round neck, placing left over right at front of sweater.

SHORT VEST TOP IN DOUBLE KNIT.

MATERIALS

Yarn (for plain vest)
5 (6 : 7) x 50g balls. D.K.

Needles
1 pair 3¼mm (UK 10)
1 pair 4mm (UK 8)

MEASUREMENTS

Bust/Chest
81/86 (91/97 : 102/107)cm
32/34 (36/38 : 40/42)in

Actual Size
100 (112 : 117)cm
39 (44 : 46)in

Length
43cm
(17in)

TENSION
22 sts and 28 rows = 10cm (4in) square
on 4mm needles (UK 8) (or size needed to
obtain given tension).

BACK
Cast on 110 (122 : 130) sts with 3¼mm
needles. Work in garter st. (every row K) for
2.5cm (1in).
Change to 4mm needles and starting with
a K row, work in st. st. Cont. straight until
work measures 10cm (4in) from beg., or
desired length to underarm, ending with a
P row.

Shape Armholes
Cast off 4 sts. at beg. of next 2 rows, and
3 sts. at beg. of next 2 rows. Dec. 1 st. at
both ends on next and foll. 5 (7 : 7) alt.
rows. (84 (92 : 100) sts.).
Work straight until armhole measures 33cm
(13in), ending with a P row.

Shape Shoulders
Cast off 6 (7 : 7) sts. at beg. of next 4 rows,
and 6 (7 : 9) sts. at beg. of next 2 rows.
Leave rem. 48 (50 : 54) sts. on a holder.

FRONT
Work as for back until armhole measures
22 rows less than back to shoulder, ending
with a P row.

Shape Neck
Next row – K33 (36 : 39) sts., turn, leave rem.
sts. on a spare needle.
* Dec. 1 st. at neck edge on next and foll. 2
alt. rows, then 1 st. on every row 12 (12 : 13)
times. (18 (21 : 23) sts.).
Work straight until armhole measures same
as back to shoulder, ending at armhole
edge.

Shape Shoulder
Cast off 6 (7 : 7) sts. at beg. of next and foll.
alt. row. Work 1 row. Cast off rem. 6 (7 : 9)
sts.
With R.S. facing sl. the next 18 (20 : 22) sts.
onto a holder. Rejoin yarn to next st. and K
to end of row.
Complete to match first side from * to end.

NECKBAND
Sew up left shoulder seam.
With R.S. facing and 3¼mm needles, pick
up and K48 (50: 54) sts. from back neck,
20 sts. from left side neck, and 18 (20 : 22)
sts. from centre front and 20 sts. from right
side neck. (106 (110 : 116) sts.).
Next row – (W.S.) K.
Next row – (R.S.) P.
Rep. last 2 rows 3 times. Cast off loosely
knitwise. Sew up right shoulder seam and
neckband.

ARMHOLE BANDS
With R.S. facing and 3¼mm needles, pick
up and K 140 sts. along front and back
armhole edge. Work band as for
neckband.

MAKING UP
Press work according to yarn instructions.
Sew up side seams including edge of
bands.

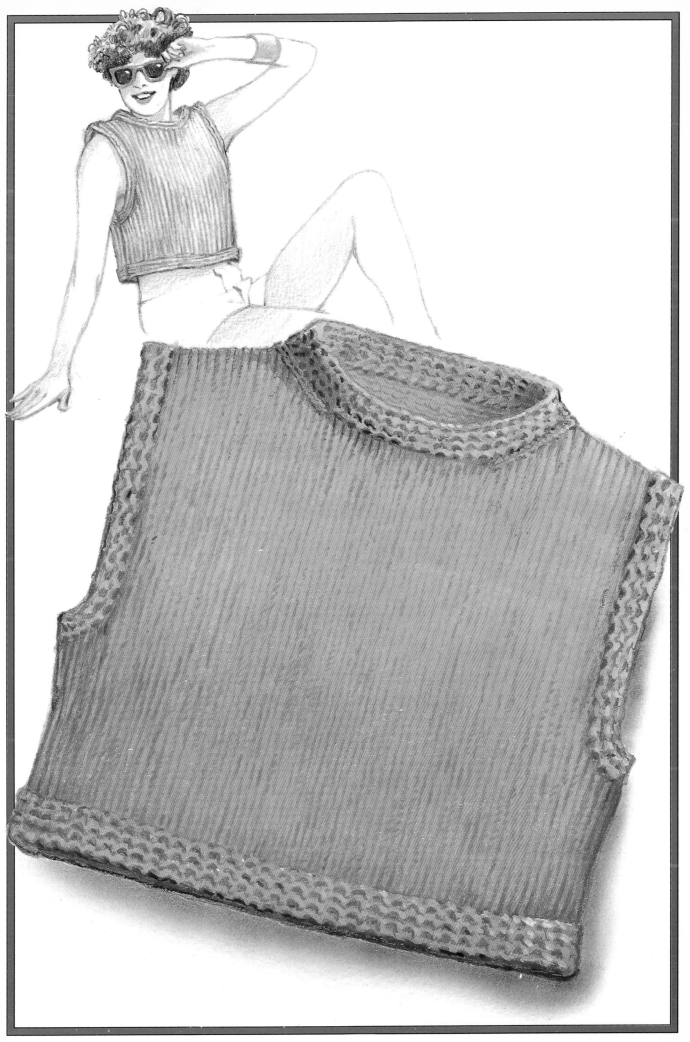

CLASSIC 4-PLY CARDIGAN.

MATERIALS

Yarn 11 (11 : 12 : 12 : 13 : 13) x 50g balls 4-ply.

Needles
1 pair 2¾mm (UK 12)
1 pair 3¼mm (UK 10)
7 buttons

MEASUREMENTS

To fit bust/chest
86 (91 : 97 : 102 : 107 : 112)cm
34 (36 : 38 : 40 : 42 : 44)in

Actual Size
91 (97 : 102 : 107 : 112 : 120)cm
36 (38 : 40 : 42 : 44 : 47)in

Length
66cm (26in)

Sleeve
46 (46 : 48 : 48 : 49 : 49)cm
18 (18 : 19 : 19 : 19¼ : 19¼)in

TENSION

28 sts and 36 rows = 10cm (4in) square
on 3¼mm needles (UK 10) (or size needed
to obtain given tension).

BACK

With 2¾mm needles cast on 124 (132 :
140 : 148 : 156 : 164) sts. Work in K1, P1 rib
for 5cm (2in). Change to 3¼mm needles
and starting with a K row, work in st. st.
Cont. straight until work measures 46cm
(18in) from beg. ending with a P row.

Shape Sides

Inc. 1 st. at both ends of the next and then
every foll. 10th row, 6 times. (138 (146 :
154 : 162 : 170 : 178) sts.).
Work 11 rows straight.

Shape Shoulders

Cast off 5 (6 : 6 : 7 : 7 : 7) sts. at beg. of
next 16 rows and 8 (4 : 7 : 3 : 6 : 10) sts. at
beg. of next 2 rows. Leave rem. 42 (42 : 44 :
44 : 46 : 46) sts. on a holder.

Pocket Linings (make 2)

With 3¼mm needles cast on 35 sts. Starting
with a K row, work in st. st. for 9cm (3½in)
ending with a K row. Leave sts. on a spare
needle.

LEFT FRONT

With 2¾mm needles cast on 62 (66 : 70 :
74 : 78 : 82) sts. Work in K1, P1 rib for 5cm(2in)
Change to 3¼mm needles and starting
with a K row, work in st. st. Cont. straight
until work measures 15cm (6in) from beg.
ending with a P row.*

Next row – K14 (16 : 18 : 20 : 22 : 24) sts., sl.
next 35 sts. on to a holder, rejoin yarn to
next st. and K to end.

Next row – P first set of sts. P across sts. of
pocket lining, P to end of row. (62 (66 : 70 :
74 : 78 : 82) sts.).

**Cont. straight until work measures 38cm
(15in) from beg. ending with a P row.

Shape Front Neck

Dec. 1 st. at end of next and every foll. 4th

row until 21 (21 : 22 : 22 : 23 : 23) front dec.
have been worked. **At the same time**
when work measures 48cm (19in) from
beg. ending with a P row,

Shape Side

Inc. 1 st. at beg. of next and then every foll.
10th row 6 times. (48 (52 : 55 : 59 : 62 :
66) sts.).
Work straight until length measures same
as back to shoulder, ending at armhole
edge.

Shape Shoulder

Cast off 5 (6 : 6 : 7 : 7 : 7) sts. at beg. of
next and foll. 7 alt. rows. Work 1 row. Cast
off rem. 8 (4 : 7 : 3 : 6 : 10) sts.

RIGHT FRONT

Work as for left front to *.

Next row – K13 (15 : 17 : 19 : 21 : 23) sts., sl.
next 35 sts. on to a holder, rejoin yarn to
next st. and K to end.

Next row – P first set of sts. P across sts. of
pocket lining, P to end of row. (62 (66 : 70 :
74 : 78 : 82) sts.).

Complete as for left front from ** to end,
reversing all shapings.

SLEEVES

With 2¾mm needles cast on 64 (64 : 68 :
68 : 72 : 72) sts. Work in K1, P1 rib for 8cm
(3¼in). On the last row inc. 44 (44 : 48 : 48 :
52 : 52) sts. evenly. (108 (108 : 116 : 116 :
124 : 124) sts.).
Change to 3¼mm needles and starting
with a K row, work in st. st. Cont. straight
until work measures 46 (46 : 48 : 48 : 49 :
49)cm, 18 (18 : 19 : 19 : 19¼ : 19¼)in from
beg. Cast off.

FRONT BAND

With 2¾mm needles cast on 13 sts. Work in
K1, P1 rib, beg. W.S. rows P1, until band is
long enough, when slightly stretched, to fit
up right front, round back of neck and
down left front to 1cm (½in) below first
neck dec.

Next row – (buttonhole row) – Rib 5 sts.,
cast off 3 sts., rib to end.

Next row – Rib to cast-off sts., cast on
3 sts., rib to end.

Mark positions on left front band for 7
buttons, the first one to match buttonhole
just worked, the last one 1cm (½in) from
lower edge and the other 5 spaced
equally between. Cont. in rib, working
buttonholes as before to match positions
marked for buttons. Work 1cm (½in) after
last buttonhole. Cast off in rib.

POCKET EDGES

Sl. the 35 sts. from pocket edge onto a
2¾mm needle and work 2cm (¾in) in K1,
P1 rib as for front band. Cast off in rib.

TO MAKE UP

Press work according to yarn instructions,
omitting ribbing. Sew up shoulder seams.
Sew in sleeves, sew up side and sleeve
seams. Sew pocket linings and top edges
in place. Sew on buttons.

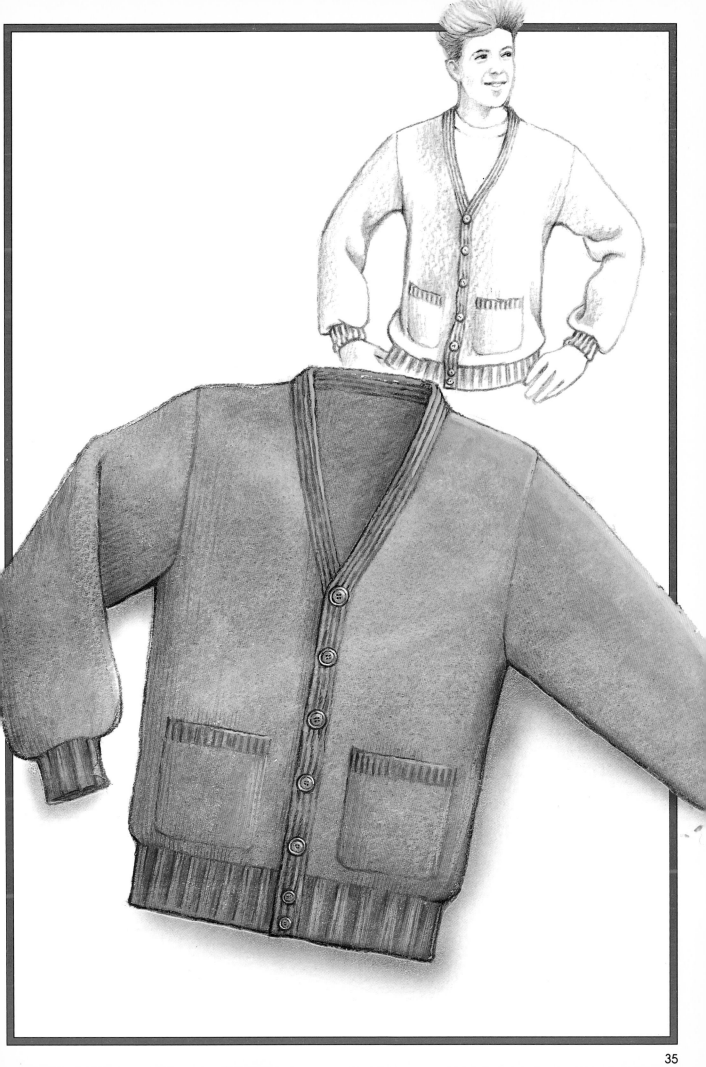

CHUNKY CARDIGAN.

MATERIALS

Yarn (for plain cardigan)
8 (8 : 9 : 9 : 10 : 10) x 100g chunky.

Needles
1 pair 4½mm (UK 7)
1 pair 6mm (UK 4)
1 open ended heavy weight zip 55 (55 :
61 : 61 : 61 : 61)cm, 22 (22 : 24 : 24 : 24 :
24)in

MEASUREMENTS

Bust/Chest
86 (91 : 97 : 102 : 107 : 112)cm
34 (36 : 38 : 40 : 42 : 44)in

Actual Size
94 (97 : 102 : 104 : 110 : 112)cm
37 (38 : 40 : 41 : 43 : 44)in

Length
65 (65 : 66 : 66 : 71 : 71)cm
25½ (25½ : 26 : 26 : 28 : 28)in

Sleeve Seam
46 (46 : 47 : 47 : 48 : 48)cm
18 (18 : 18½ : 18½ : 19 : 19)in

TENSION

15 sts and 18 rows = 10cm (4in) square
on 6mm needles (UK 4) (or size needed to
obtain given tension).

BACK

Cast on 66 (69 : 72 : 75 : 78 : 81) sts with
4½mm needles. Work in K2, P1 rib for
7.5cm (3in).
Change to 6mm needles and starting with
a K row, work in st. st. Cont. straight until
work measures 43 (43 : 43 : 43 : 46 : 46)cm,
17 (17 : 17 : 17 : 18 : 18)in from beg.
ending with a purl row.

Shape Armholes

Cast off 4 (5 : 5 : 6 : 5 : 6)sts. at beg. of next
2 rows. Dec. 1 st. at both ends on next
3 rows. (52 (53 : 56 : 57 : 62 : 63) sts.)
Work straight until armhole measures 22
(22 : 23 : 23 : 25 : 25)cm, 8¾ (8¾ : 9¼ : 9¼ :
10 : 10)in, ending with a purl row.

Shape Shoulders

Cast off 6 (6 : 6 : 6 : 7 : 7) sts. at beg. of
next 4 rows, and 6 (6 : 7 : 7 : 7 : 7) sts. at
beg. of next 2 rows. Cast off rem. 16 (17 :
18 : 19 : 20 : 21) sts.

POCKET LININGS (make 2)

With 6mm needles cast on 18 sts. and work
2.5cm (1in) in st. st., ending with a
P row. Leave sts. on a spare needle. Make
another one the same, but ending with a
K row.

LEFT FRONT

**With 4½mm needles cast on 33 (33 : 36 :
36 : 39 : 39) sts. Work in K2, P1 rib for 7.5cm
(3in).
Change to 6mm needles and starting with
a K row, work in st. st. for 4cm (1½in),
ending with a P row.**

Divide for Pocket

Next row – K9 (9 : 12 : 12 : 15 : 15) sts.
K across 18 sts. of first pocket lining.
(27 (27 : 30 : 30 : 33 : 33) sts.). Leave rem.
24 sts. on a spare needle.
Working on first set of sts., turn and starting
with a P row st. st. 21 rows.
Next row – K9 (9 : 12 : 12 : 15 : 15) sts, cast
off rem. sts. Leave sts. on a holder.
With R.S. facing rejoin yarn to rem.
24 sts. on spare needle at base of pocket
opening and starting with a K row st. st.
23 rows.
Next row – P24 sts. then P across 9 (9 : 12 :
12 : 15 : 15) sts. on holder. (33 (33 : 36 : 36 :
39 : 39) sts.).
Cont. in st. st. and work straight until front
matches back to armholes ending with a
P row.

Shape Armhole

Cast off 4 (5 : 5 : 6 : 5 : 6) sts. at beg. of
next row. Work 1 row. Dec. 1 st. at armhole
edge on next 3 rows. (26 (25 : 28 : 27 : 31 :
30) sts.). Work straight until front measures
58 (58 : 59 : 59 : 63 : 63)cm, 22¾ (22¾ :
23¼ : 23¼ : 24¾ : 24¾)in from beg. ending
at front edge.

Shape Neck

Cast off 2 sts., P to end of row.
Dec. 1 st. at neck edge on next 5 (4 : 5 : 4 :
5 : 4) rows, then 1 st. on foll. 1 (1 : 2 : 2 : 3 :
3) alt. rows. (18 (18 : 19 : 19 : 21 : 21)sts.).
Work straight until length measures same
as back to shoulder ending at armhole
edge.

Shape Shoulder

Cast off 6 (6 : 6 : 6 : 7 : 7) sts. at beg. next
and foll. alt. row. Work 1 row. Cast off 6 (6 :
7 : 7 : 7 : 7) sts.

RIGHT FRONT

Work as for left front from ** to ** but
ending with a K row.

Divide for Pocket

Next row – P9 (9 : 12 : 12 : 15 : 15) sts.
P across 18 sts. of second pocket lining.
(27 (27 : 30 : 30 : 33 : 33) sts.). Leave rem.
24 sts. on a spare needle.
Working on first set of sts., turn and starting
with a K row st. st. 21 rows.

continued

Next row – P9 (9 : 12 : 12 : 15 : 15) sts., cast off rem. sts. Leave sts. on a holder.
With W.S. facing rejoin yarn to rem. 24 sts. on spare needle at base of pocket opening and starting with a P row st. st. 23 rows.
Next row – K24 sts., then K across 9 (9 : 12 : 12 : 15 : 15) sts. on holder. (33 (33 : 36 : 36 : 39 : 39) sts.).
Complete to match left front reversing shapings.

SLEEVES
With 4½mm needles cast on 36 (36 : 39 : 39 : 42 : 42) sts. Work in K2, P1 rib for 7.5cm (3in).
Change to 6mm needles and starting with a K row, work in st. st. inc. 1 st. at both ends on 4th and foll. 4th row 1 (1 : 1 : 1 : 2 : 2) times, then every foll. 6th row until there are 54 (54 : 57 : 57 : 62 : 62) sts. Work straight until sleeve measures 46 (46 : 47 : 47 : 48 : 48)cm, 18 (18 : 18½ : 18½ : 19 : 19)in from beg. ending with a P row.

Shape Top
Cast off 4 sts. at beg. of next 2 rows. Dec. 1 st. at both ends of next and every alt. row until 24 (24 : 25 : 25 : 28 : 28) sts. rem. Dec. 1 st. at both ends of every row until 12 (12 : 13 : 13 : 14 : 14) sts. rem. Cast off.

FRONT BANDS (both alike)
With 4½mm needles and R.S. facing pick up and K83 (83 : 86 : 86 : 98 : 98) sts. along front edge.
1st row – P2,* K1, P2, rep. from * to end.
2nd row – K2,* P1, K2, rep. from * to end.
Rep. these 2 rows once more, then 1st row again. Cast off loosely in rib.

COLLAR
Join shoulder seams. With 4½mm needles and R.S. facing pick up and K24 (24 : 25 : 25 : 27 : 27) sts. from right side neck, 20 (20 : 21 : 21 : 23 : 23) sts. from back neck and 24 (24 : 25 : 25 : 27 : 27) sts. from left side neck. (68 (68 : 71 : 71 : 77 : 77) sts.). Work ribbing rows of front bands until collar measures 10cm (4in) from beg. ending with 2nd row.
Next row – P2 tog., rib to last 2 sts., P2 tog.
Next row – Rib all sts.
Rep. last 2 rows twice more. (62 (62 : 65 : 65 : 71 : 71) sts.).
Next row – P2 tog., rib to last 2 sts., P2 tog.
Next row – K2 tog., rib to last 2 sts., K2 tog.
Rep. last 2 rows twice more, then 1st row again. (48 (48 : 51 : 51 : 57 : 57) sts.).
Cast off loosely in rib.

POCKET EDGES
With 4½mm needles and R.S. facing, pick up and K20 sts. from side edge of pocket. Work 5 rows in K2, P1 rib as for front bands. Cast off in rib.

MAKING UP
Press work according to yarn instructions omitting ribbing. Sew in sleeves. Sew up side and sleeve seams. Sew pocket linings in position to W.S. and sides of pocket edges to R.S. Sew in zip.

Abbreviations
D.K. – double knitting
g – gramme(s)
cm. – centimetre
in(s) – inch, inches
mm – millimetre
K – knit
P – purl
st. st. – stocking stitch (1 row knit, 1 row purl)
cont. – continue
beg. – beginning
st.(s) – stitch(es)
rem. – remaining
tog. – together
alt. – alternate
dec. – decrease
foll. – following
W.S. – wrong side
R.S. – right side
col. – colour(ed)
inc. – increase
patt. – pattern
sl. – slip
rep. – repeat

Humour

What to include in this section was not exactly a problem but since I am forever being accused of having a schoolboy sense of humour I allowed the editor to have the last word. You, of course, won't have him looking over your shoulder, so be as daft or as rude as you like.

Chosen, in the end, was this selection of slightly dotty images. Some motifs like the 'T.V.' set and 'Banana' are everyday things, but putting them on clothing does, for one reason or another, make me smile – I don't know that I have ever seen a T.V. set on a sweater before!

The 'Queen of Hearts' vest is a design I thought anyone could tackle and the 'Home Sweet Home' speaks for itself. You must surely know someone who would be mildly offended to receive this one as a surprise gift.

The 'Polka Dot' bow is a rather glamorous variation on the clothing jokes I am often asked to do. Try out belts and braces, bow ties, school ties, cameras and binoculars round your neck, waistcoats, evening suits – I am sure you can add to this list yourself.

Last but not least the 'Hot Dog' design. No section on knitted humour would be complete without a bit of food slopped down a sweater. There is no need to stay at the hamburger level, if you are really ambitious, go for the whole three course dinner.

HOT DOG
4 ply sweater.

41

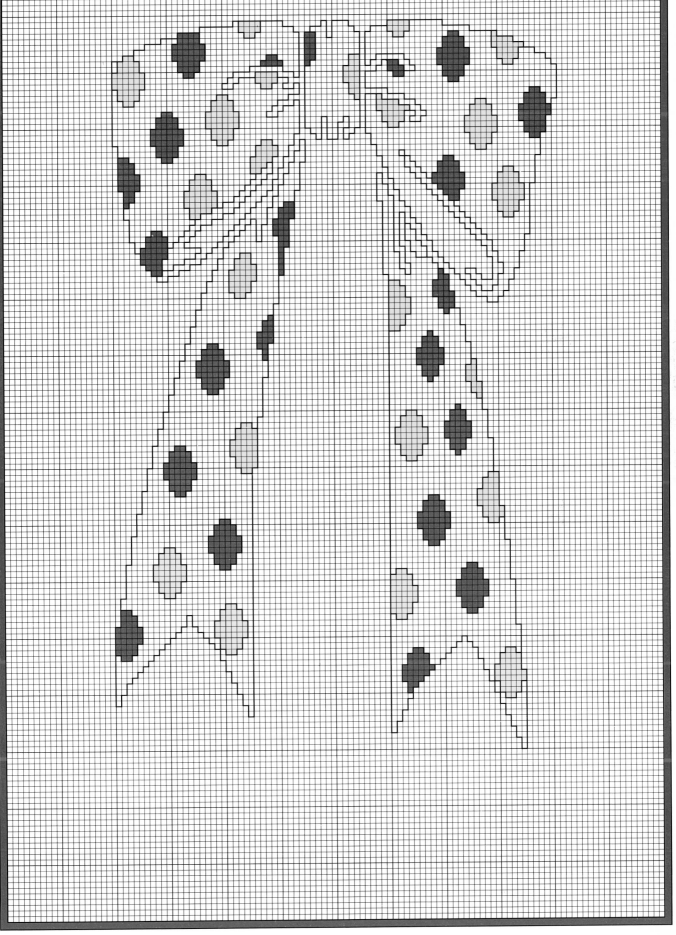

POLKA DOT
4 ply sweater.

43

QUEEN OF HEARTS
D.K. vest.

BANANA
Chunky cardigan.

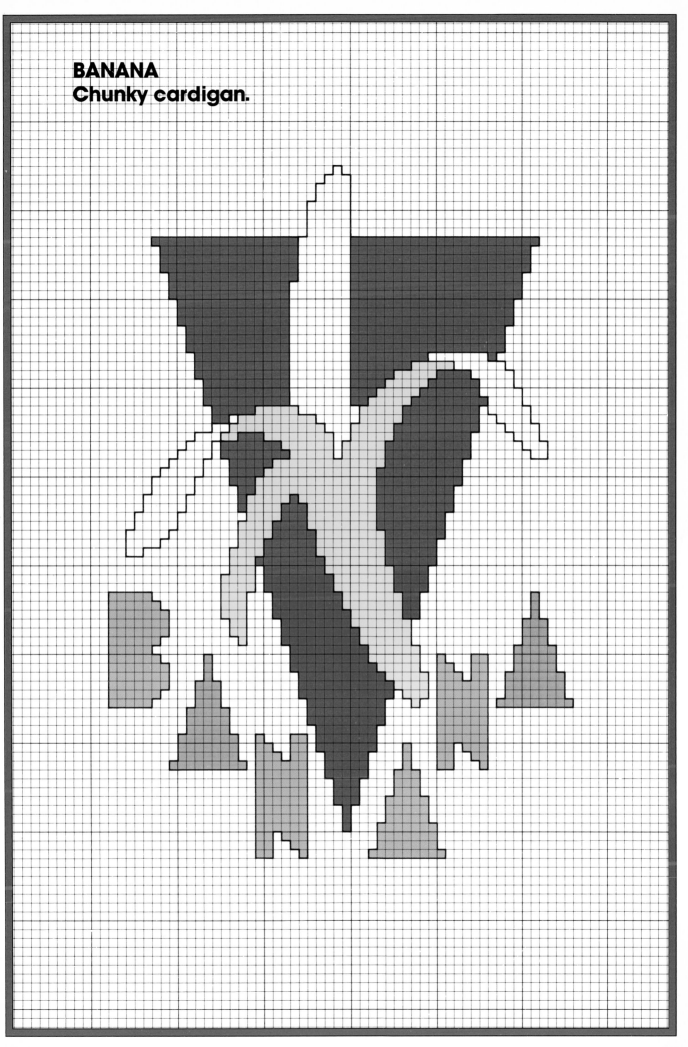

HOME SWEET HOME
D.K. slipover.

T.V. SPECTACULAR
D.K. vest

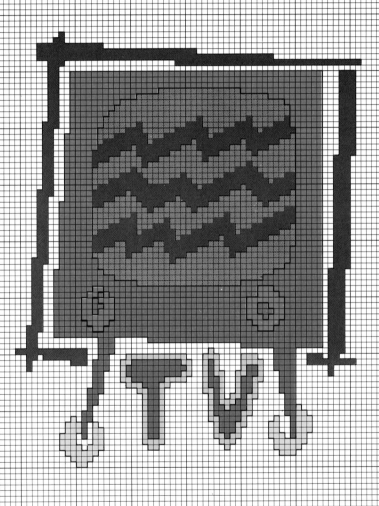

your own graph

Pet owners, I am told, end up looking like their pets – well, get yourself off to a flying start.
On the next few pages are a selection of ideas you might like to work from.

The well fed 'Tabby Cat' may be a little tame for you, in which case go for the 'Big Cat'.
You should be someone's pet dressed in that one.
The 'Spaniel' is included as a representative of the canine world. Over the years I have been
commissioned by many proud owners and breeders to design sweaters to show off their
dogs. They are an ideal subject for picture knitting, since once you have the outline worked
out you can add the markings of your own family pet making it instantly recognisable
to anyone who knows you.

Children, of course, often form greater attachments to cuddly toys rather than the real
live thing. You could raise a few smiles by reproducing a favourite plaything on the front
of a knatty knit.

The list of possibilities is, of course, endless. I have tackled drawings for cows, horses, sheep,
snakes, rabbits, hedgehogs, mice, hamsters, bees, parrots, cockatoos, owls, frogs, etc., etc.
On one memorable occasion I was presented with close up shots of a breeder's favourite
tarantula which he emblazoned on sweaters for the whole family.
Your taste in pets may not be quite as esoteric as that, but you could be the
first person in your street with a stick insect cardigan.

BIG CAT
D.K. sweater.

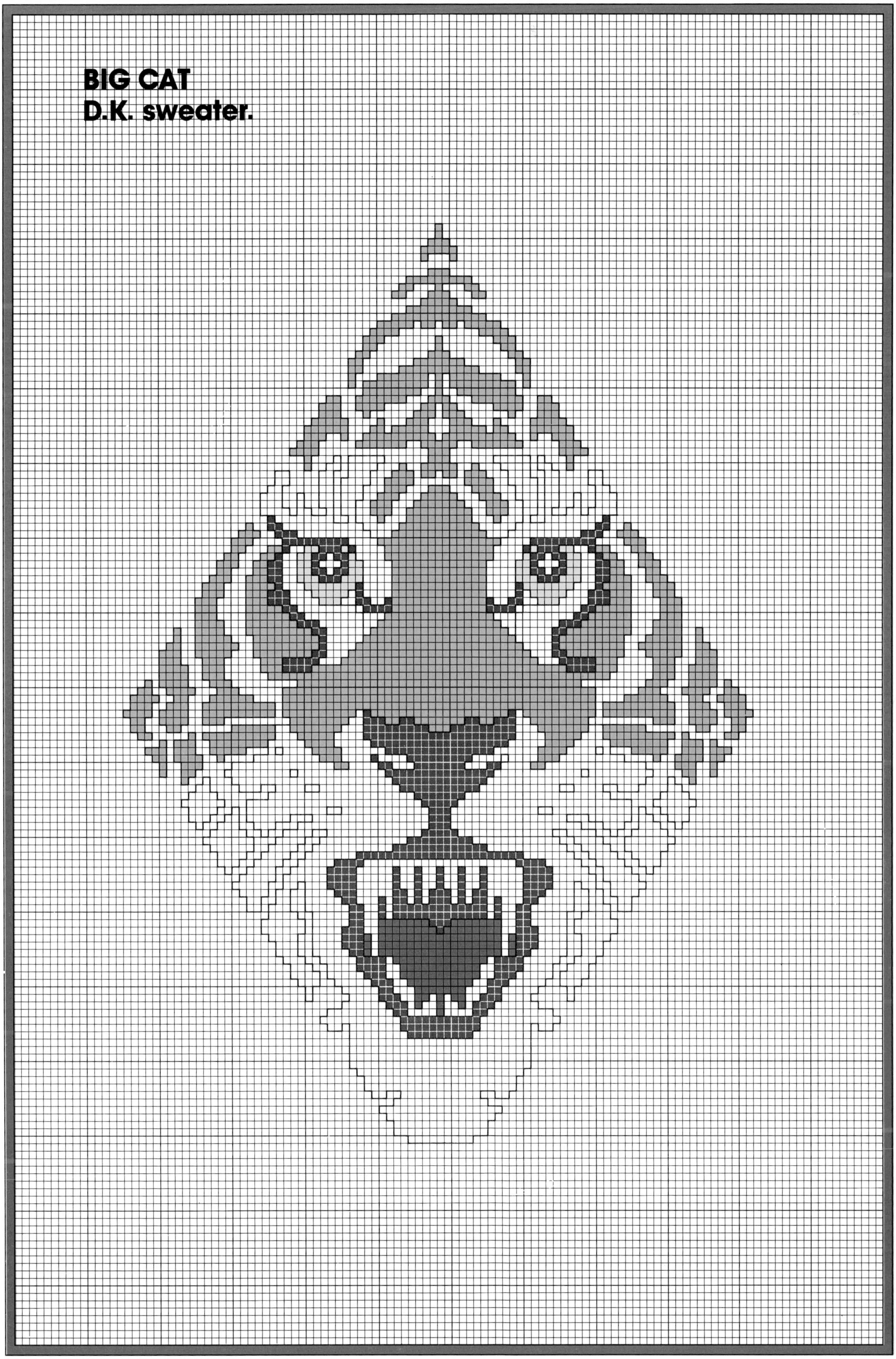

TEDDY
4 ply sweater.

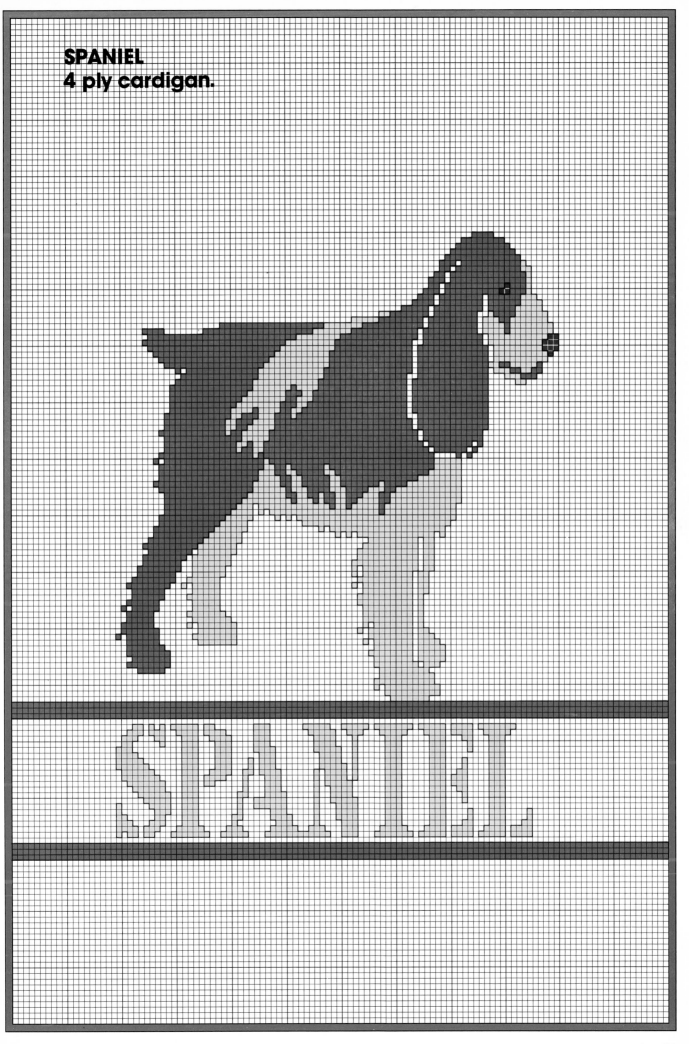

SPANIEL
4 ply cardigan.

TABBY CAT
4 ply sweater.

your
own graph

Any teenager will recognise the 'Stereo' radio among this selection of designs, but you might gave to guess the age of anyone who asks you to knit the 'Juke Box'. For me, Pop still conjours up good old rock 'n' roll, and I couldn't resist drawing out, yet again, a variation on the theme.

Pop music imagery is certainly in plentiful supply. There are more books, magazines, comics, not to mention album covers, than any other area of visual communication. You will be able to find plenty of examples of musical instruments like guitars, drums, trumpets, violins etc. – I have included a piano and saxophone.

Move your ideas on into dance crazes, from tap to break dancing. Patent leather shoes and top hats to graffiti and trainers. Disco decor with zapping lazers and abstract themes provide spectacular material for your knitting enterprises.

On the 'Jazz' illustration I have added a few music notes to the sleeves, but I leave it to you to 'flash up' your sweater as you like. Pop isn't, of course, just the world of music. I have included a 'Custom Car' in the selection, but you might just as easily tackle your own favourite speedster – or clapped out banger as the case may be.

Keep on knitting!

BOOGIE WOOGIE
D.K. slipover.

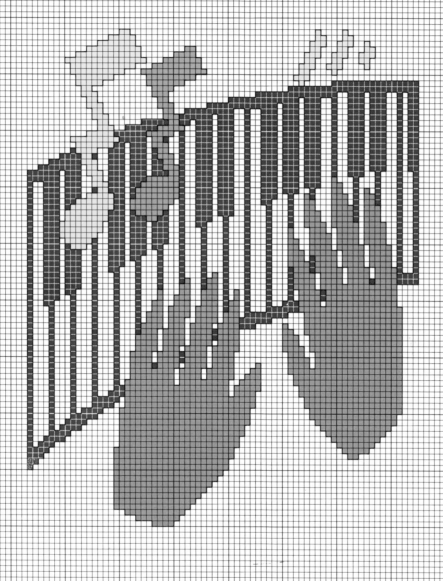

COOL JAZZ
4 ply sweater.

STEREO SOUNDS
D.K. sweater.

HOT ROD
4 ply cardigan.

ROCK 'N' ROLL
D.K. vest.

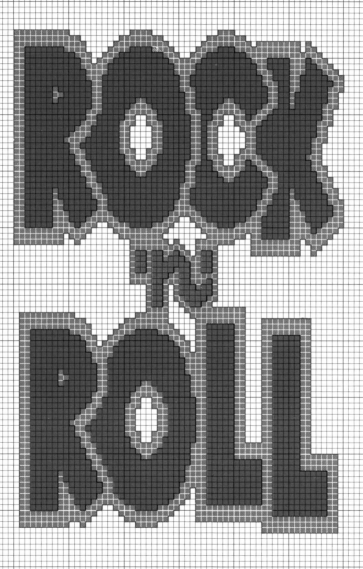

JUKE BOX JUMP
Chunky sweater.

your
own graph

Heroes

We each have our own heroes. Though you may not belong to any fan club, there will always be some charismatic performer who will tempt you into the cinema or a star who gets you in front of the T.V. set for the evening.

I chose Marilyn, Elvis and Groucho for personal nostalgic reasons but you will, of course, have your own particular idols. In the case of the last design, well, I threw that in for the odd megalomaniac who might think they could be another Superman. I suppose you could have some fun inventing your own super-hero badge and then getting out to save the world.

The three personalities I have drawn have each been treated in a different artistic manner. Catching a likeness in knitting is not always easy, so use the techniques I have shown here as examples. In the case of the Groucho drawing the fact that he has a moustache, glasses, a cigar and a bizarre hair style make the task much simpler. Where your model has no particular extreme features, then try to catch a typical pose or gesture to make the finished work that much more convincing. If you are in real trouble, stick the name underneath using the alphabets illustrated later in the book.

THE KING
D.K. sweater.

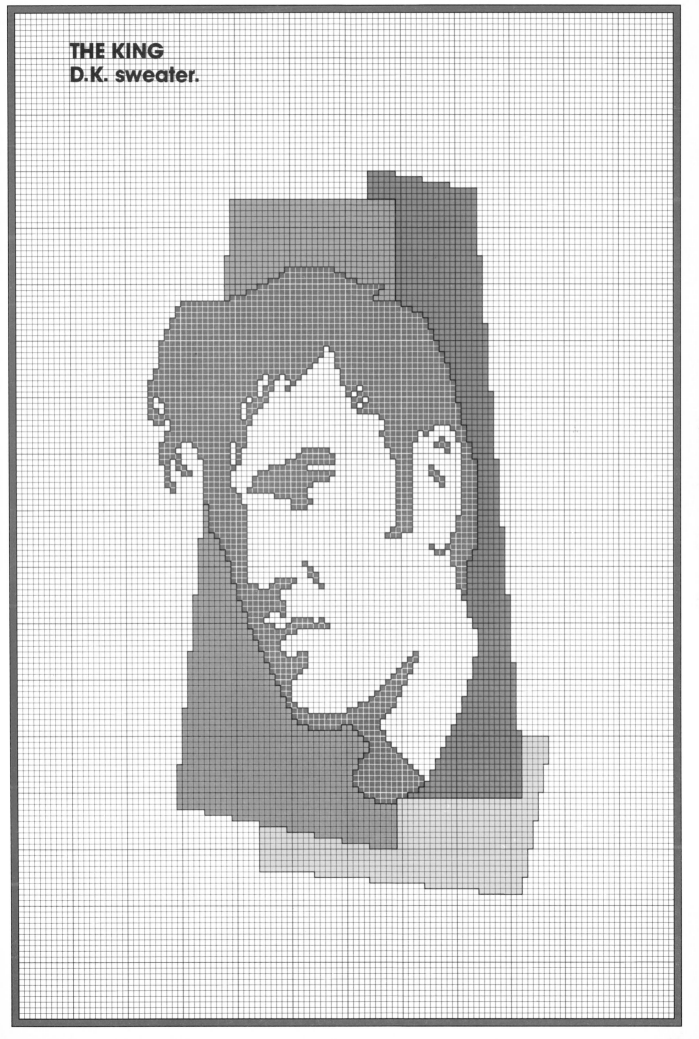

MARILYN
Chunky cardigan.

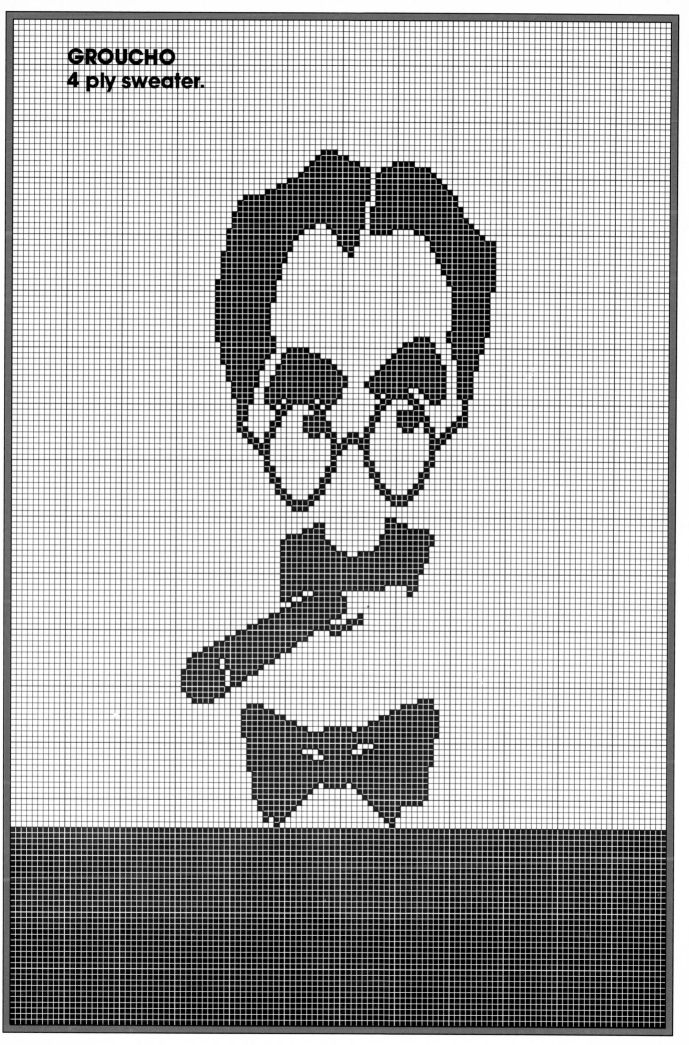

GROUCHO
4 ply sweater.

SUPER HERO
4 ply sweater.

your
own graph

Sporting sweaters have long been a popular item and it is quite likely that if you have been knitting for any length of time you will have tackled some sort of sports orientated garment. I hope this book will enable you to spread your wings a little and come up with some really striking designs.

In the examples included, I have avoided the usual football, golf and skiing images which you can find in other sources. Instead, I have tried to extend the range just a little to indicate how wide an area you have to explore.

The 'Boxer' is there simply because I have never seen one on a sweater before but if you have a heavyweight friend risk it as well as trying out body builders, weight lifters, circus strong men, etc.

The 'Tennis Player' is a fairly classic theme, but I kept it casual with long trousers. In any event bare legs are very difficult to make look handsome in knitting, so bear that in mind when tackling a design of your own.

Motorcycling magazines are a wonderful source of action packed pictures. The very nature of the sport makes any related design look heroic. I am sure if you completed the sweater illustrated here or one which you have worked up yourself, you will find you have knitted a crowd stopper.

New sports and crazes seem to crop up all the time. Skateboarding then B.M.X. cycling, surfing now wind surfing, have all appeared in the last few years as popular pastimes or competitive sports. You may not windsurf yourself but that shouldn't prevent you from knitting the example included here.

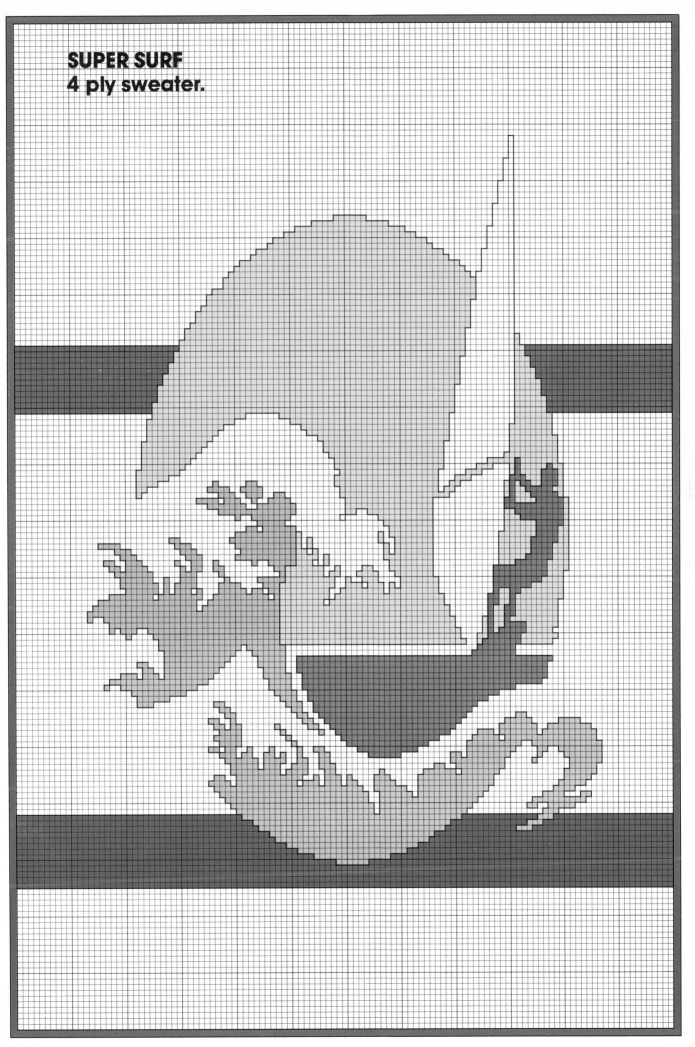

SUPER SURF
4 ply sweater.

ANYONE FOR TENNIS?
4 ply sweater.

KNOCKOUT
4 ply sweater.

POWERBIKE
4 ply sweater.

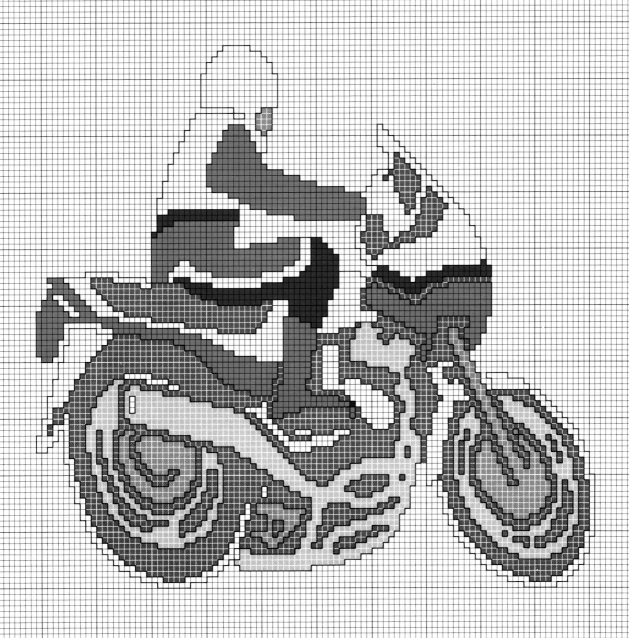

your own graph

Star signs are included as a theme mainly because of the surprising volume of requests
I receive for designs of this sort.

You will find a couple of pages of astrological signs as examples for you to work from.
It is impossible to produce graphs for all twelve signs without giving over a whole book
to the theme (there's an idea) but the examples shown should give you
a direction in which to proceed.

The actual signs themselves are fairly straightforward. The samples are almost all solid,
silhouette outlines. The words could be made up from the alphabets to be found on
later pages. A star sign sweater could certainly be a good starting point
if you haven't tried picture knitting before.

I am told that each sign has a particular colour associated with it, but I think I will let you do
your own research on that one. Who knows, perhaps someone will cross your palm with
silver for one of your creations? Good luck!

TAURUS THE BULL
4 ply sweater.

LEO
D.K. vest.

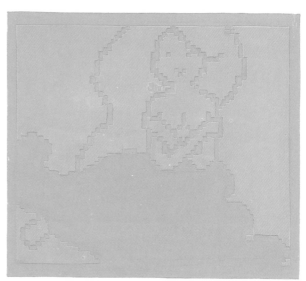

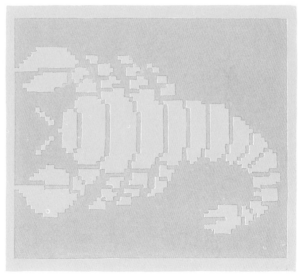

your own graph

Special Events

Creating sweaters for special events, occasions and celebrations take up a considerable amount of my time as a knitwear designer, whether it be for winning yacht crews or a T.V. station's first anniversary. The Olympics, The Admirals Cup, The New York Marathon, The F.A. Cup, The Super Bowl, Rock concerts, Crufts dog show, The Eurovision Song Contest have, among others, all been events which have required me to sit over the drawing board and come up with a 'knatty' range of designs. However, on the home front make a start with birthdays and Christmas. These are probably the two most important events in everyone's calendar, at least until you get to around my age, in which case just settle for Christmas. I have drawn out a scrumptious 'Birthday Cake' and a 'Christmas Tree' as starting points – add more candles as the years roll by.

The 'Wedding Bells' might just be wishful thinking for someone or, in a leap year, a broad hint. A matched pair of sweaters could cut a fine dash at your next escorted appearance at a society wedding.

Holidays are an event in themselves and I have included a 'Cruise' design for your perusal but, again, adapt the theme for your own delight. Try the Eiffel tower on your return from Paris or London Bridge, the Taj Mahal, The Pyramids – the world's your oyster!

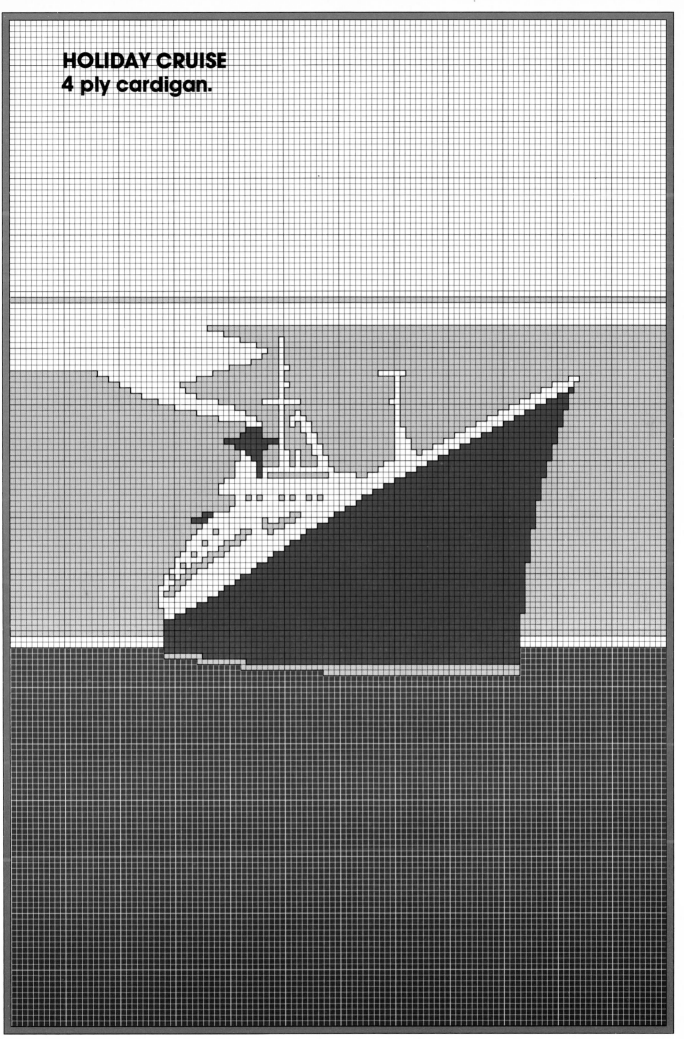

HOLIDAY CRUISE
4 ply cardigan.

HAPPY BIRTHDAY
4 ply sweater.

WEDDING BELLS
4 ply sweater.

MERRY CHRISTMAS
4 ply sweater.

your
own graph

Alphabets

Lettering seems to cause a considerable amount of trouble for the amateur designer – and the professional, for that matter. I have drawn out four alphabets of varying styles so that you have a reasonable choice to match the yarn you will be using or the style of design you are attempting. After a little experience you will see that handling letters is much the same and can be just as rewarding as drawing out an elegant picture.

Use the alphabets to add names, initials, jokes or personal messages to your knatty knits. You will find them easy to follow, but do draw them out again for your own design. Don't try to follow them letter by letter from the printed graph straight onto your knitting. Each letter must be placed next to its neighbours with some care. Don't just leave the same gap of one or two squares between each letter. If, for example, you have a capital 'T' next to an 'A', squeeze the 'T' against the 'A' so that the top of the 'T' overlaps into the box of space taken up by the 'A'. Arrange your letters by eye with this spacing principle in mind for the most balanced, satisfactory results.

When using the cursive 'handwriting' script, draw out the letters as shown then extend and add to each letter enough squares or stitches to join the letters in a convincing manner.

You may, of course, wish to recreate your own alphabets and letters. In this case treat them as pictures and as outlined in the book, look for examples to work from.

For particular styling of words as in the 'Jogger' sweater, spend some time drawing the words freehand then apply the 'squaring up' technique described in an earlier section.

Whatever you choose to do, make it fun.

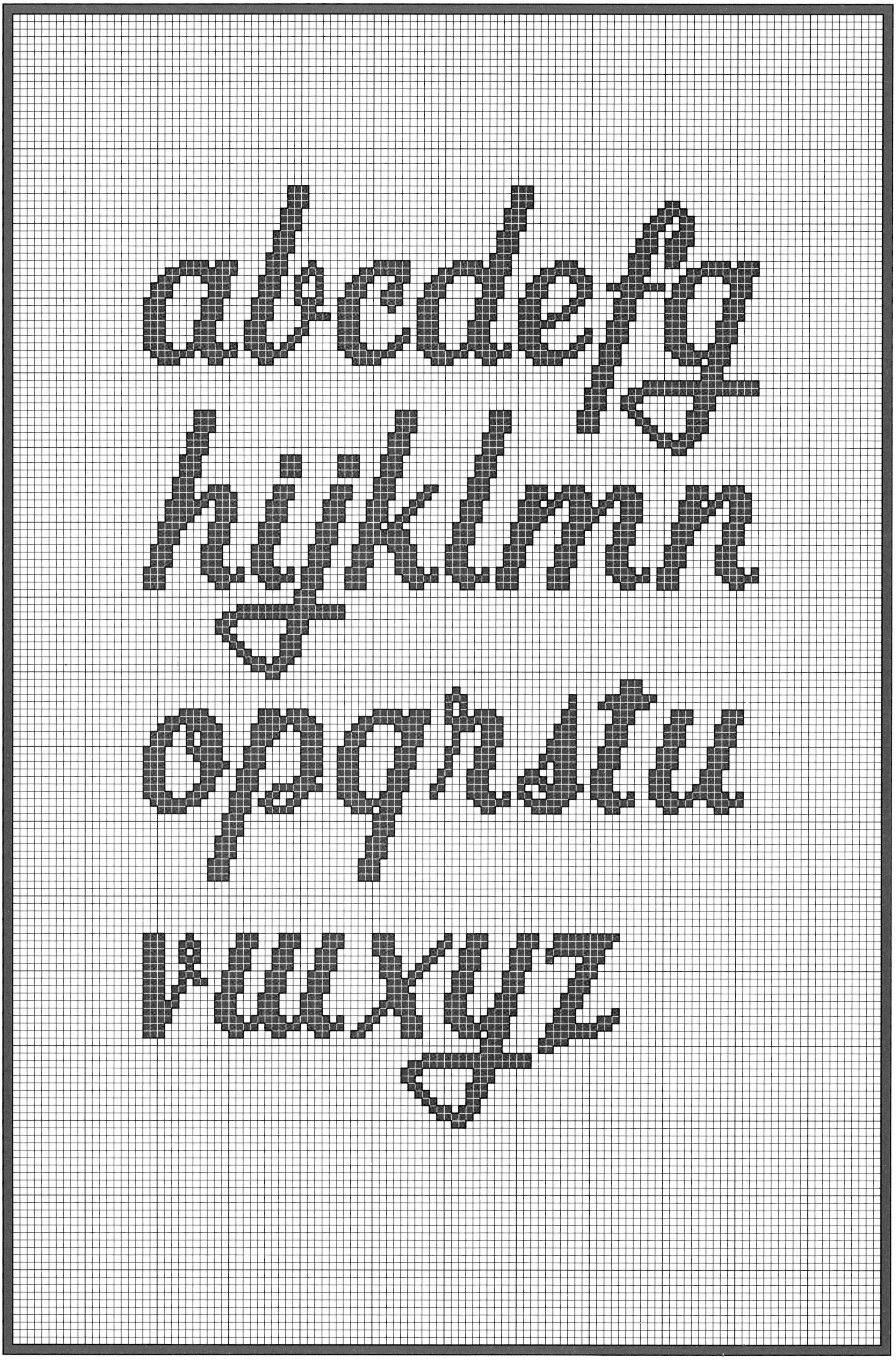
abcdefg
hijklmn
opqrstu
vwxyz

abcdefg
hijklm
nopqrst
uvwxy
z

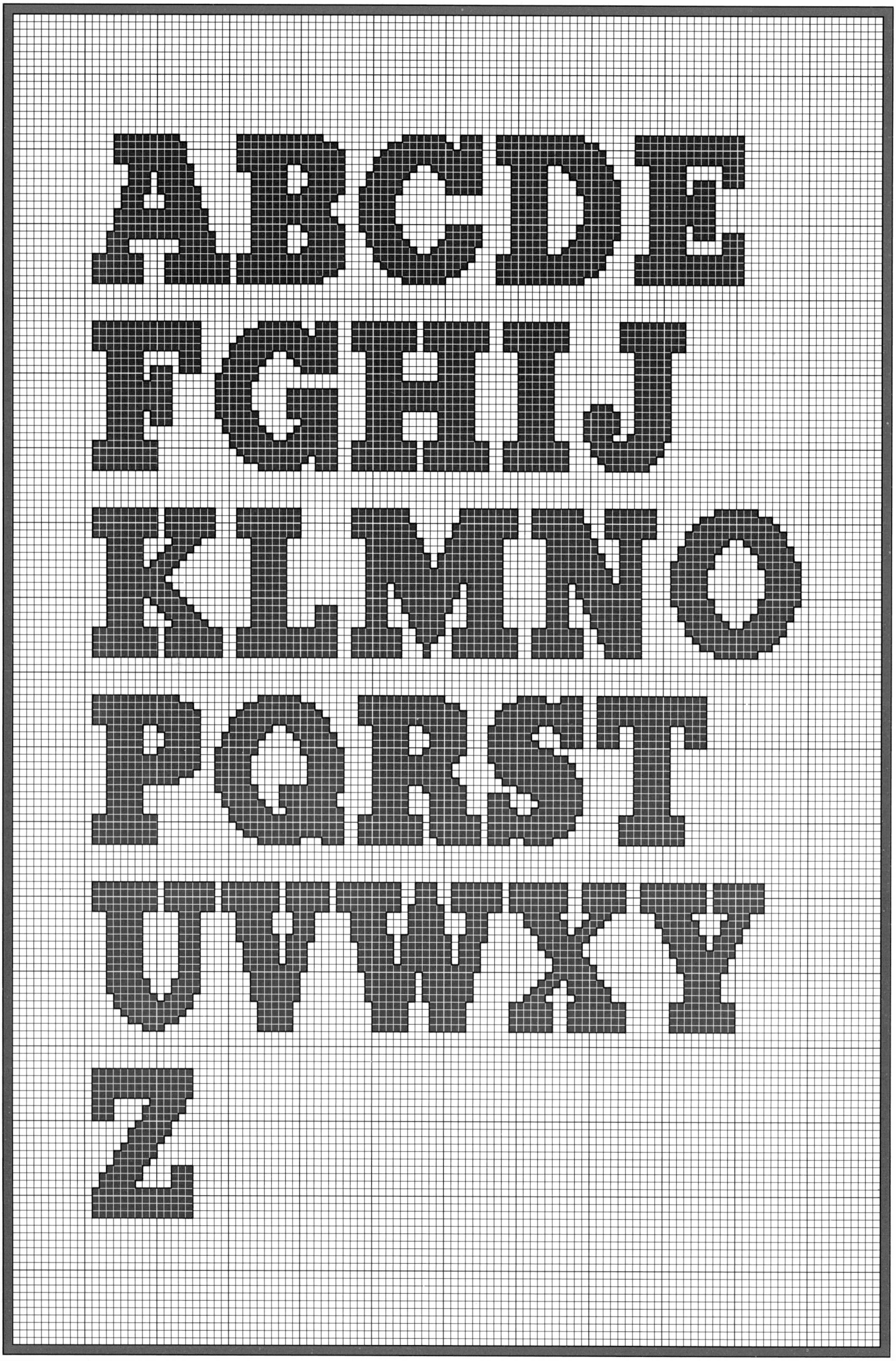
ABCDE
FGHIJ
KLMNO
PQRST
UVWXY
Z

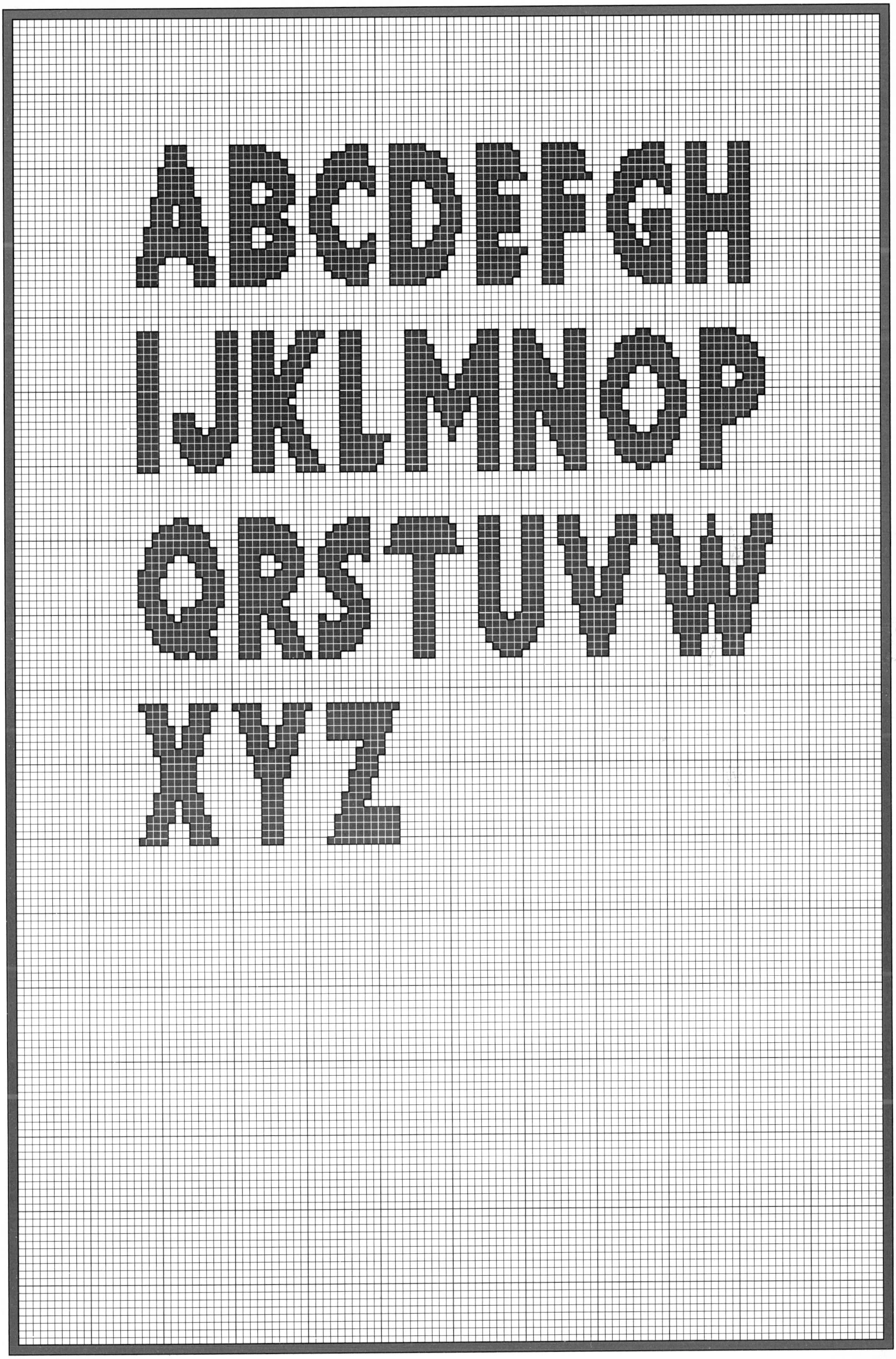
ABCDEFGH
IJKLMNOP
QRSTUVW
XYZ

your own graph

your own graph

your own graph

your own graph